SECOND EDITION

POLICE OFFICER
TO
ENTREPRENEUR

THE SIX-STEP METHOD FOR BUILDING A SUCCESSFUL BUSINESS BEYOND THE FORCE

ALEXANDER SEERY

Praise

Alex is certainly one of those leaders in life who inspires people to achieve greater things, and police officers will be no different. His six-step methodology gives key stepping stones in building a successful business. This book is a truly thought-provoking one that generates mindset shifts, and is an absolute must read for anyone who is wanting to transform their lives to become their own boss in the ever-expanding world of entrepreneurship.

Simon Zutshi – Author of *Property Magic*, international speaker and founder of the property investors network

Officer turned six-figure entrepreneur, Alex shares practical yet simple techniques to give you the confidence to take a leap of faith in becoming your own boss. At a young age, Alex has demonstrated that you can turn your life around within a short period of time. This book is a must read for any police officer who wants to break free from the force and live a life full of freedom, recognition and financial reward.

Kunal Dattani – E-commerce entrepreneur, founder and company director, Mo Bro's

My dad was in the Essex Police Force for twelve years, but I always got the impression that he would have been content with a salary of double what he was getting. In reading Alex's book, I realised my dad was missing this vital blueprint to move from serving police officer to entrepreneur. Alex's book is perhaps three decades too late for him, but it's not too late for you. This is a great resource. Embrace it.

Robin Waite – Business coach and author of
Online Business Startup and *Take Your Shot*

Alex is living proof that his six-step methodology to building a successful business works. The book will help any new entrepreneur not only to develop a successful strategy but also to develop that critical mindset required to build the business of their dreams. It would have certainly saved me a lot of valuable time when I moved from a lifetime in the police service to running my own business. I know that I could have benefited from this wisdom. I thoroughly recommend anybody wishing to move into working for themselves to read this powerful book and benefit from the knowledge that Alex has accrued over his life as a business owner.

Kul Mahay – Author of *Smash the Habit*, *The Immersion Coach* and international speaker

For most people, deciding to leave the comfort zone of long-term paid employment like the police force to start your own business can feel like a daunting if not risky task. Alexander Seery has not only successfully done that himself but is helping others do the same. This book provides a clear blueprint to help the reader lock down their business idea and safely transition into self-employment. In addition to his practical, no-nonsense, six-step methodology, Alex provides sensible, first-hand advice that will lead, inspire, and give you the grounded enthusiasm and confidence to succeed.

Andrew Priestley, Grad. Dip. Psych. – Award-winning business leadership coach, and bestselling author of *Starting*, *The Money Chimp* and *Awareness*.

I left the police service after 10 years of being married to the job. It was a struggle to adapt to any other job, however I realised business was the way to go. It took me 3 years of job-hopping to identify my transferable skills from the police service and implement them into my entrepreneurial journey, but with the help of this book you can do it much quicker than I did. I've said this time and time again: If I had had access to the skills and training that Alex delivers through Shifts to Success, it would have made my transition more manageable – and easier to swallow for my family.

Steven Thompson – Social media expert, speaker, founder and CEO of BIGDaddy PR social media agency.

Contents

Part 3: Entrepreneur Essentials

*This book is dedicated
to the policing family,
past and present.
Thank you.*

Foreword

In a perfect world, this book would never have been written. As a young detention officer, Alex Seery would have enjoyed every minute of his career knowing that he had a respectable income, the resources he needed to do his job and support from government and the community.

Instead, Alex met with the realities of today's police service – chronic underfunding, income that doesn't even keep up with inflation, a lack of support from government and a community preoccupied with their latest smartphones rather than civic duty.

Alex shared with me the moment he decided enough was enough. A detainee had defecated all over himself and his holding cell; Alex was sent to assist the detainee, but found himself having to restrain the large, violent man covered in faeces as he tried to escape his cell. Later, wiping the muck off his hands and face, he decided this was it – there simply wasn't enough respect, income or security in the police service to warrant these kinds of experiences.

Alex started a property development company whilst working full time. Within three years, he was able to more than triple his police income and has gone on to become a successful and highly respected entrepreneur.

What he discovered was a world of opportunity that he had actually been given great training for. His police training comprised of skills that every entrepreneur needs – discipline, curiosity, endurance, building rapport, establishing authority and working in trusted teams.

His passion is to give police officers choices, so that if ever they've had enough they have a path to a completely new life. The book you have in your hands walks you down that path and covers all the key questions you might be asking about the entrepreneurial world and whether you could achieve your ambitions as a business owner.

Rather than diving straight into the ins-and-outs of setting up a business, Alex spends time building a case for entrepreneurship as a career. He thoroughly answers the questions many police officers want to know, before even thinking about a new business.

He does this from a perspective very few people have – an ex-detention officer who is now a successful entrepreneur. He has also inspired other ex-police officer entrepreneurs to share their stories for your encouragement and guidance.

As someone who's worked with thousands of entrepreneurs and built several businesses myself, I can assure you that you are in for an exciting ride if you choose to grow a business. Building a business is both challenging and fun. Done right, it gives you meaningful work, quality relationships and disproportionate rewards.

In a perfect world, you wouldn't be reading this book. The title wouldn't have jumped out at you, the idea of leaving a police job to start a business wouldn't seem appealing, and your friends and family would never understand why you'd want to read a book about starting a business. Yet here we are at a time where this book is highly relevant and desirable to any police officer – the book has been written and you've discovered it for a reason. Some people will actually be relieved to see you are exploring other options. Hopefully, if enough police officers start looking elsewhere, the government and the community will have to put a higher value on the police service.

Regardless of what happens at a macro level, let's begin your entrepreneurial journey. I wish you all the success you deserve in business and in life, and I thank you for your dedicated service to the community as a police officer, and hopefully as a business owner too.

Daniel Priestley
Entrepreneur and best-selling author
Founder and CEO of Dent Global

Introduction

More and more police officers are becoming less passionate about their roles. They spend time away from their families and loved ones, they feel undervalued and underappreciated, all while facing horrific and dangerous situations on a regular basis. This causes unhealthy amounts of stress.

However, it does not have to be this way. Police officers who are unhappy in their current roles can have a successful career away from the service by becoming entrepreneurs and building their very own successful businesses.

If you are a police officer looking for an alternative path to provide you with more time to do the things you love to do, more income so that you're truly rewarded for your efforts, and without the unwanted stresses of the job, then this book will show you exactly how to find that path. Start to live life on your own terms.

Police Officer to Entrepreneur will guide you through three sections. Part 1 concentrates on the reasons why I believe police officers can seriously consider entrepreneurship as an alternative career path.

Part 2 concentrates on my Shifts to Success Business Builder Model (Ideas, Planning, Branding, Implementation,

Products and Sales), which will give you all the practical information you need to help you get your business up and running.

Part 3 covers the essentials you'll need as an entrepreneur: mindset, energy and execution. These will help prime you for your entrepreneurial endeavours, energise you for the exciting journey ahead, and spur you into action.

Within the book, you will discover some inspirational case studies from former colleagues Steven, Dionne, Kul and Rick who have made the transition into entrepreneurship successfully and have all achieved financial independence, generating incomes in the six figure range. Not only that, but in Part 2 of this book, you'll discover success stories from our clients at Shifts to Success, Katie, Chris, Victoria, Jamie, Kelly and Lorna, who have all gone on to transform their lives.

There has never been a greater time in history to build a business of your own as an entrepreneur. Technology has greatly levelled the playing field, removing barriers and opening up thousands of potential business options, many of which still haven't been explored. A great idea is the best starting point in developing your own business, but an idea alone won't get you very far. You need to be clear on how to generate entrepreneurial ideas that are fun and respectable, understanding different niche markets and how to validate your ideas so you can piece together inspiring concepts to progress forwards.

Once you have your idea, *Police Officer to Entrepreneur* will guide you through the other steps in the Shifts to Success Business Builder Model, accelerating you towards a sustainable, profitable business. The model will give you new insights on how to develop your business idea and clarity on how to plan it correctly, implement your plans, develop a strong brand, create amazing products and generate rewarding sales. As a result, you will be able to build a business from scratch in an industry you enjoy, accelerating you towards being financially independent and giving you another opportunity in life with freedom and choice.

I realise police officers are sworn in and serve the Queen, and as such do not have the same rights as employees. However, for the purposes of this book, I will refer to police officers as employees.

I want you to have fun reading this book, but remember that the real fun only begins when you take action to create a life of your dreams. My hope is that this book not only inspires you, but also changes your belief system. The life you envision for yourself is very much possible. Your unique success may be closer than you think.

So let's start your journey, and I'll be backing you all the way.

PART 1

The Entrepreneur In You

Chapter 1

Why Is Now the Best Time to Become an Entrepreneur?

'To any entrepreneur: if you want to do it, do it now. If you don't, you're going to regret it.'

Catherine Cook

Key learning points from this chapter:

- The old way of thinking
- The new way of thinking
- The barriers have been removed
- The benefits of being an entrepreneur
- How entrepreneurs are helping the world
- The lifestyle business
- Your undervalued skillsets

The old way of thinking

The world is changing at an alarming rate. The path to a successful life used to be: go to school, go to university, get good grades, work your way up the career ladder, pay your bills, then end up with a good pension to provide you with an income until you die.

The big issue around this way of thinking is that it takes too much time to climb the employee ladder, and if you dislike the job you're in, you may end up bitter, resentful and unfulfilled.

From the age of seventeen, all I ever wanted was to become a police officer. I was told it was a good, rewarding, respectable job, I would never be made redundant, I would experience new things each day, and the job came with amazing benefits, including a great pension. Not to mention chasing down bad guys.

At the age of twenty-three, I joined the police as a special constable. I committed to twenty-two weekends of training and was so excited to wear a police uniform. Full of optimism, I was due to turn up at the police station to await my first day of being mentored by a serving police officer. I couldn't sleep the night before due to my mind running wild, imagining all the exciting things I would be doing.

I arrived bright and early the following day at what I can only describe as an old, fusty shed. It reminded me of a school warehouse where teachers and students store their PE equipment. The floor was filthy, and there was a large table in the centre of the main room covered with paper and documents, peppered with dirty coffee and tea mugs. There were also around six computers that looked like they were from the Stone Age.

The whole building was a hideous mess, but what was more discomforting was the atmosphere. The police officers in the station were not smiling much; there would be the odd occasion where some banter would fly around, but to be honest, the officers I came into contact with didn't seem to want to be there. They couldn't wait to clock off shift, saying, 'Only two more hours to go, woohoo!' Something wasn't right. When something feels 'off', that's usually because something *is* off! If you are unhappy with how your life is unfolding as a police officer and are looking for other options, the only way to find your perfect match is to create something that you believe in; something that you can work on; something that isn't dictated by policy; something that you can control 100%.

There has never been a better time to start your own business and become successful at it, and it all starts with a new way of thinking.

The new way of thinking

In 2014, I joined the police service as a detention officer based in custody. By 2015 I was financially independent, achieving an income of £62,000 p.a. from my business in the property industry. I had built this business while working in the service, and its income more than doubled my police salary. I didn't have unhealthy stress; I had passion. I felt valued, and now I had the choice whether to resign from my role in the police, which would provide me with more time than I would know what to do with.

How did I achieve an income equivalent to that of a superintendent? I rejected the old way of climbing the ladder of success as an employee and welcomed the new way of thinking. I made my own rules as an entrepreneur.

Today, the world rewards ambitious, calculated risk-takers who know how to make things happen for themselves and provide value in the service of solving other people's problems.

The barriers have been removed

In the old days, people needed hundreds of thousands of pounds to get a business up and running. These days, we have the internet. It's free, and it has all the knowledge we will ever need to build a successful business. It is the implementing of that information which is the hard part.

The barriers that were once there have been removed. Seize this incredible opportunity and live a rewarding life you truly want for you and your loved ones. To gain amazing things from your own business is very much possible. Success isn't reserved for the special few; it is there for anyone who grabs an opportunity and takes massive determined action.

But why take action to become a successful entrepreneur in the first place? As with all things, business success may not be for everyone. That is why I highly recommend you take the police officers' scorecard quiz at www.shiftstosuccess.com.

The benefits of being an entrepreneur

I am passionate about entrepreneurship because I know what is possible, and I find successful people fascinating. My mindset has made amazing shifts over the years due to the content I have consumed through business events, seminars, workshops and programmes, not to mention the hundreds of books I have bought and read.

When I was working as an officer based in custody, I knew that some day that I would resign from that role and run my own business. I just didn't realise how fast that would happen. When I actually made the transition into entrepreneurship full-time, I discovered a whole heap of awesome benefits in addition to having more money.

Below I have listed ten of these benefits.

1. Freedom. This is one of my favourite benefits. As an entrepreneur, I have complete freedom to live where I want, earn as much as I want, work with whom I want and allocate my time where I want. I don't have to worry about clocking on and off shift, booking in annual leave, or even getting called in on my rest days.

If you are an entrepreneur, your agenda is your own. No one dictates your life; you choose your working hours as well as your destiny. Entrepreneurship *is* freedom.

2. Age doesn't matter. I worked out the math. For me to reach a salary of £145,000 as a chief constable, I would have to be in an age range of forty to fifty, not to mention all the stresses I would have had to go through to reach such a rank. However, at the age of twenty-six, I achieved an income of £110,000pa within two and a half years of starting my business, and it continues to grow.

Age doesn't matter in the world of entrepreneurship. Mark Zuckerberg, the co-Founder of Facebook, became the youngest billionaire in history at the age of twenty-three. In contrast to that, Colonel Sanders, the founder of KFC, built up his billion dollar company at the age of eighty-eight. Age is seriously just a number when you are an entrepreneur.

3. Profits over wages. Whatever rank you reach in the police service there will be a cap on the amount of money you can earn. To make matters worse, you have to trade your time to earn your wage. However, as a business owner, you can create and leverage systems within your business to ensure you are not trading your time for money. You can even make money while you sleep.

4. No politics. New polices, software, changes in processes, even which political party is in government can shape your destiny as a police officer. In achieving a certain rank, you have to follow a process that the organisation sets out for you. As an entrepreneur, you make your own policies and processes, and can change them whenever you feel like it.

5. No sacking or suspensions. As an entrepreneur, no one can sack or suspend you. You may get complaints from your customers, but these are opportunities to learn and improve your business.

6. You are never bored. An entrepreneur always has something new and exciting around the corner, because they are in control. Entrepreneurs launch products, bring team members on board, create branding, make business deals, and write books. Some can work from anywhere in the world, perhaps looking over a gorgeous view with a cocktail in hand.

In the world of entrepreneurship, boredom doesn't exist, because you get to do what *you* want to do.

7. You get paid your worth. As an entrepreneur, you find your true worth. If you're earning £4,000 a month, you can increase that to £1 million per year through innovation, progress, effort and self-improvement as there is no cap on your earnings.

Personally, I think police officers should be paid way more than they currently are paid, because they deserve more for all their efforts.

> Police officer turned entrepreneur Steven Thompson, the founder of BIGDaddy PR, was earning £35,000 p.a. working up to eighty or ninety hours a week in the police service. Yet in the first year of starting his business, he was earning £50,000 p.a., and it only took him eight months to establish a sustainable income. Four years on, his business is producing a six figure income, which is continuing to grow.

8. Creativity. One of the most amazing things I have come to realise since becoming an entrepreneur is that I am in fact a creative person. I didn't know this when I was working in the service because I had no opportunity to express my creativity, but now my mind is running wild with different planning ideas, marketing ideas, product concepts, events, and sales strategies. I've even written my own book. I was so fixed in my mindset when I was working in the police that I wasn't aware of my capabilities.

9. Constant personal growth. Are you constantly growing as a police officer? Are you celebrating new achievements, hitting new targets and goals or pushing the boundaries of what you're capable of?

Being an entrepreneur, I am always in a state of personal development. I am constantly learning about my character, my mindset, new strategies, new concepts, new ways of implementing tasks, new partnerships to reach higher levels for my business and personal life. In his book *Secrets of The Millionaire Mind*, T. Harv Eker states, 'If you are not growing, you are dying', and I completely agree. As soon as I adopted this mindset, I ensured that I would constantly grow, and I could not be happier.

10. Legacy. In the last ten minutes of your life, what thought do you believe will be running through you mind? Will it be a feeling of achievement? Will it be memories of a life fully lived? Will it be a feeling of gratitude?

I am twenty-seven years old at the time of writing this and I am hopefully many years away from dying. But when that day comes, I won't be saying, 'I wish…' I don't want to die with regrets running through my heart and mind. Instead, I will be thinking of all the special moments I spent with my family and loved ones, the quality of our lives, the contribution I made to charities and helping other people around the world, and the impact I made in helping police officers become successful entrepreneurs.

Remove 'I wish' from your life.

I am always intrigued by the benefits that ex-police officers have found in building their own business. A close friend Rick Gannon, who was a serving police officer for ten years, is now a successful entrepreneur, investor and author. His top three benefits are:

1. Freedom of being able to work for myself
2. Being able to help more people than I ever helped while in the police force
3. Construct a thriving business that I can leave to my children

I asked Rick to tell his story leading up to leaving the police service.

I arrived home at around 7.30am after a night shift dealing with a sudden death. Feeling a little despondent and tired, I walked into the kitchen and greeted my wife Lorraine and then went upstairs to kiss my children, a ritual I always followed after a night shift.

My five-year-old daughter Charlotte was her usual happy self, but my nine-year-old son Ben was looking troubled.

'Hey, Ben, are you okay?' I asked.

'No, not really, Dad,' he replied. 'I'm worried about something.'

'Okay, what is it? Maybe I can help.'

Ben then said something that would be the catalyst for me re-evaluating my life and making a total change.

'Dad, why can't I play football like my friends?'

Wow, this was a total sucker punch. You see, Ben had been born almost three months premature and has Quadriplegic

Cerebral Palsy. He has no use of his legs at all and only limited use of his arms, and is dependent on around the clock care from Lorraine and me. I honestly didn't know how I could answer this, but I'm his dad. I had to make this right.

'It's okay, Ben, we will find a way,' I said, with a lump in my throat.

Lorraine at the time worked from home as a procurement consultant. We had a discussion about life in general and I told her about my shift and how depressing it had been. We then spoke about Ben and how we could help him achieve his goal of playing football. That was when I knew I needed to leave my job as a police officer.

Rick has never looked back since. As a police officer, he loved to make a difference in helping his community, but now he is helping even more people throughout the UK with his successful business. New Era Property supports newbie property investors, and that is what all great entrepreneurs do – they help people. Rick has now also set up an incredible wheelchair football team, so that his son can now play football.

How entrepreneurs are helping the world

I was dropping a friend off one day when the most amazingly beautiful car passed by. It was a Lamborghini Aventador, my all-time favourite car. I couldn't stop staring at it, and my imagination went insane with thoughts of owning one.

However, something my friend said caught my attention, which is pretty hard to do when a car that beautiful is going by. He said, 'Self-centred git'. I just ignored the comment at first, but as the day went on, I began to think more and more about it. I then googled the term 'self-centred' and found, 'preoccupied with oneself and one's affairs'.

I just didn't agree at all with my friend's comment. The person driving that car was clearly successful, but so many people get conditioned from a young age to think that wealthy people are just out for themselves. In a lot of cases, nothing could be further from the truth.

Entrepreneurs are successful because they help and serve other people.

A few famous examples:

TONY ROBBINS. According to his website, he has, through his partnership with Feeding America, provided over 200 million meals to those in need in the last two years, and he is on track to provide a billion of those meals by 2025. He also provides fresh water to 100,000 people a day in India to prevent waterborne disease, which is the number one killer of children in that country.

ELON MUSK. Through his company SpaceX, he designs, manufactures and launches advanced rockets and spacecraft. His company wants to revolutionise space technology, with the ultimate goal of enabling people to live on other planets. His company Tesla is helping accelerate the world's transition to sustainable energy.

BILL GATES. Through his company Microsoft, Bill Gates wanted to see a computer on every desk and in every home. He and his wife Melinda also head up the influential Bill &

Melinda Gates Foundation. In 2007 alone, the Foundation spent over $2 billion on global education and health initiatives. None of these people started off wealthy. They wanted a better life for themselves in the service of helping other people around the world. I don't care if you are selling bean bags to primary schools, nutrition plans to the elderly or advice on how to train a dog, as an entrepreneur, you are helping and serving other people, providing value to them, and you're being paid for doing so. So next time you see someone in a flashy car, wearing a lovely suit or showcasing their brand new watch, know they have those rewards because they have provided value to someone through their business.

Detective constable-turned-entrepreneur Dionne Buckingham-Brown adds value by supporting her clients to target their ideal customers with precision using social selling, and in the process increases their sales. As an entrepreneur, she solves a problem through her service, and she deservedly gets paid for doing so.

There are many paths you can take in building your own business, but I would recommend building a lifestyle business.

The lifestyle business

A lifestyle business is set up and run by its founders primarily with the aim of sustaining a particular level of income, or to provide a foundation from which to enjoy a particular lifestyle. This is the type of business I would encourage police officers to build towards, mainly because there is less stress and more freedom involved than when you're starting up a huge company. Just look at the first step you need to take, and then the next, and so on, and sooner or later you'll have achieved your goals.

I now want to go into more depth on why building a lifestyle business is much more rewarding than trying to build the next Facebook, Apple or Google.

You are not creating another job. One of the main benefits of being in business is that it provides you with freedom and flexibility to do what you want, when you want, where you want, and with whom you want. With a huge company start-up, this doesn't tend to happen. You don't get the benefits you signed up for as an entrepreneur.

You hit profit much sooner. With a huge start-up company, you can wait years to hit profit. This isn't a good thing, especially when you are trying to leave the police service. You'll want profit much quicker than that.

When you build a huge company, you will need investors or the bank to provide you with start-up capital for resources such as staff, equipment, distribution and other necessities. When you take on this loan, you are going to have to pay it back, with interest, before you touch any profit.

> *'If you are starting a business and you're taking out a loan, you are a moron. Most small businesses fail due to a lack of effort.'*
>
> Mark Cuban, billionaire entrepreneur
> in an interview for *Bloomberg*

Less stress with a lifestyle business. There will be less stress involved in building a lifestyle business than there is working in the police service, but there will be much more stress involved in starting a huge company. When creating a lifestyle business, you don't have to worry how you are going to pay your employees or if your revenue is 37% lower than what you'd anticipated. You don't have to stress about your investors or partners having different ideas on how your business should unfold. In a lifestyle business, you don't have to answer to anyone. You are in the driver's seat.

The side hustle. If you are thinking, *I can't start a business when I am working full-time in the police service,* stop right there. One of the points I teach police officers is to use the side hustle method. You can work on your business after you have clocked off shift and on your rest days. You do not have to quit your job until your business reaches a sustainable level of income.

Location. A huge benefit of creating a lifestyle business rather than a huge company is that you are not restricted by location. This is great for police officers who have a family as they can work from the comfort of their own home, and it's also great for those who love to travel as generally all they need is an internet connection.

No employee overheads. www.peopleperhour.com, www.fiverr.com, www.freelancer.com and www.upwork.com are amazing websites, offering freelance services that allow you to create your own team, depending on what kind of work you need help with, without the need to hire someone and put them on a salary. These websites help you outsource your workload to someone better suited to the task than you for a reasonable price. And they are found all around the world. My personal videographer is based in London, my digital designer is in India, my PDF creator is in Russia and my virtual assistant is in South Africa.

When you build a lifestyle business, you don't need employees who can potentially cause big issues and big business expenses. You can quite easily use the websites mentioned above to find someone who will fit each role at a much cheaper price.

These benefits are attractive to many people throughout the world, but not all people have the skillsets that you as a police officer already possess.

Your undervalued skillsets

Let's get into five skills that police officers already possess that will help them succeed in business as an entrepreneur.

1. Effective communication. Being a police officer, you have to communicate effectively with fellow colleagues, the public and the courts, verbally and in written format. You do this on a day to day basis.

A lack of communication internally and externally can lead to the collapse of any business. Without proper marketing, most businesses will struggle to survive. Communication can also lead to productivity, which helps avoid unnecessary delays in the implementation of your amazing entrepreneurial ideas.

Next time you are on shift, look around you and listen to your colleagues. Notice the damn good job you all do of communicating effectively, which could be transferred into building your own successful business.

2. Assertiveness. Without a doubt, you as a police officer will come into contact with some unsavoury people from time to time. Each time, you need to show some level of assertiveness to take control of the situation.

Assertiveness is a skill that many successful entrepreneurs have too. Assertiveness can take you far in the business world as it describes how you defend your interests. Assertive entrepreneurial leaders can create a compelling vision, communicate business strategies and clearly define objectives and service quality standards. They inspire their people, gather support, and create alignment within a team so that everyone moves in the same direction. They avoid the confusion and disorientation caused when team members are trying to second-guess what they're supposed to be doing.

3. Problem solving. When you look back on your career, I bet there have been some instances where you have faced a frustrating problem and have used your mindset to pull in the support of colleagues and solve that problem. Being an entrepreneur is essentially all about problem solving. Every problem is an opportunity to grow your business, come up with innovative ideas and spark a passion you never knew was there.

4. Team working. When I was based in custody dealing with violent detainees, there was always at least one cop, either female or male, who showed incredible team working skills. They would communicate ideas, plan and take action to deliver an outstanding result where everyone was safe, including the violent detainee.

I remember on one occasion dealing with a female detainee who was crying so much I didn't know what to do. A female police officer came to my assistance without hesitation and dealt with the matter superbly. This is a great example of team working, which is such an important skillset to have when starting, sustaining and scaling a business. Team working is about pulling in resources to deliver a desired end result. Being an entrepreneur, you will need to grow your network, and when this grows, so will your ability to work in a team with some amazing entrepreneurial minds.

5. Resilience. Police officers have an incredible ability to bounce back after encountering difficulties on duty, and this unique skill of mental toughness can be transferred into the business world as an entrepreneur. Resilience enables people to move through hardship and become better. To be happy, successful, bold and humble requires resilience, a quality that police officers have already developed through their service. Resilience is a powerful tool to become successful in the world of business as an entrepreneur.

These five skillsets are just a few of the many you as a police officer already possess. I hope this encourages and inspires you to believe not only in your ability to succeed in business, but also in your own unique value. I believe you are more than a police officer; you are an entrepreneur waiting for an opportunity to achieve success.

Summary

We have covered a lot of ground in this opening chapter, and I want to congratulate you. You now know way more than the general public about entrepreneurship and business.

We have gone through why the world is rejecting the old way of thinking and adopting the new way of thinking, which will help you reach success quickly. In this day and age of the internet, it is easier than ever to start a successful business and reach a global market. We've looked at ten reasons why being an entrepreneur beats being a police officer, and how entrepreneurs serve communities on a broad scale. We've covered what type of business to create to provide you with an amazing lifestyle and the skillsets you already possess to help you become a successful entrepreneur.

In the next chapter I will obliterate the myths about being an entrepreneur so you can start taking steps towards a life you truly want.

Chapter 2

Myths of Being in Business

'*Myths are a waste of time. They prevent progression.*'

Barbra Streisand

Key learning points from this chapter:

- Be careful whom you take advice from
- Following your passion isn't necessary to achieve success
- You don't need to be a genius
- Entrepreneurship isn't a lonely journey
- You don't need lots of cash to start your business
- You don't need to know everything about business to get started
- You don't have to be an extrovert to run a business

In this chapter, I want to dispel six common myths you may hear about being an entrepreneur and business owner.

These myths can slow you down if you are thinking about starting your own business or wanting to scale your business, or, even worse, stop you from taking any action at all.

I actually used to believe in these six myths, told to me by people who weren't even successful in business. There are people all around who will freely give advice when they have no idea what they are talking about. If an overweight guy or girl was giving me advice about a healthy nutritional diet plan, I would politely reject that advice. The same should go for business advice.

Be careful whom you take advice from

When I was twenty-one, I sought the advice of a financial advisor in my bank. He told me all about how to invest and save money to create 'real' wealth, and because I was curious and a little cheeky, I asked, 'Do you do these things?'

It caught him off guard, and he stuttered, 'No, but...'

In that moment, I politely wrapped up the meeting. He wasn't in a position to be giving me advice when he wasn't even implementing the things he was telling me to do.

From the books I have read over the past six years on business, wealth creation and entrepreneurship to the seminars, workshops and programmes I have attended, to my mentors who are multi-millionaire entrepreneurs, to the highly successful millionaires I have interviewed – that's the kind of advice I want. If you want to be a public speaker, learn from a public speaker; if you want to be a bus driver, learn from a bus driver; if you want to be a successful entrepreneur operating your own business, learn from a successful entrepreneur operating their own business. Learn from people who really understand the problems you will face. On our business accelerators, I get highly successful mentors who are specialised in each area of the Shifts to Success Business Builder Model to teach valuable content to police officers.

So now you know to be cautious of who you take advice from, let's look into the six common myths around entrepreneurship and business.

Following your passion isn't necessary to achieve success

You will hear these phrases a lot, especially from wannabe entrepreneurs: 'Do what you love' or 'Follow your passion', like they're some secret to success. The problem is that people misinterpret this advice. If you do follow your passion, you are less likely to give up, regardless of the result, because you love what you're doing. And that can keep you broke for a long time, which is not exactly a great strategy for success.

You do not have to be passionate about something to be successful. I can seriously say I am not passionate about property and refurbishments in the slightest, but despite this, I achieved great results in this industry, one of which was financial independence. The thought of not having to work for someone else again *did* excite me, and that's very important to note. My property business was just a vehicle for me to attain that.

If you are anything like me, you may end up thinking too

deeply about your 'passions' and coming to the conclusion you aren't passionate about anything. Or perhaps there is something you are passionate about, but you wouldn't want to go into business for it. For example, I love sausage dogs, but I wouldn't want to build a business around them. Does that mean I should call it a day and get a job? Hell, no!

Another issue around following your passion is that if you are not actually good at doing the thing you're passionate about, you can miss out on a lot of opportunity.

If you have a passion that you can create a business around, great. Go for it. But for those of you who haven't, I would advise starting a business to create a lifestyle for yourself then find out what your passions may be.

By looking at the data from police officers who have taken the scorecard quiz at shiftstosuccess.com, I can see that 66% are passionate about the police service. But unfortunately, there are also many things they dislike, which far outweigh their passion for the job. For example, 97.3% said they would like the freedom to choose where they work; 93.4% stated they want more out of their life; 83.7% said they enjoy their rest days more than their working days; 77.9% stated they do not feel appreciated for their efforts in the job; 97.4% stated they want to improve their income; 83.5% stated they are highly stressed in the job; 93.6% stated they would like to be in control of the hours they work; 94% stated they would like opportunities to help people with their own business; and 86.7% stated their jobs are having a negative impact on their family and home life.

Passion can become a trap that stops you from breaking out into something that may serve you and your loved ones better. Just because you are passionate about something doesn't mean you should remain with it for the majority of your life, because what you may be passionate about now can soon turn into a dislike. Plus in the business world, market needs will always triumph. The market doesn't care about your passion; the market cares about what it needs.

> '*Insanity is doing the same thing, over and over again, but expecting different results.*'
>
> Albert Einstein

Are you doing the same things within your life and expecting different results? Your life won't get better by chance; it gets better by change.

I had to change one of my brands, Ultra-Preneur®. Even though I loved what I was doing, interviewing highly successful millionaire entrepreneurs, an adjustment was needed because the business model wasn't great. It wasn't producing a decent return on investment.

If you do not have a passion, I would recommend you work on building a business in an area that at least interests you or grabs your curiosity. An oak tree starts as a tiny acorn, and this acorn represents curiosity. What grabs your curiosity? What do you spend money on regularly? What can you lose yourself in doing? What interests you? What excites you? The answers may hint at where you can grow your little acorn of curiosity into an oak tree of a business with unshakeable roots.

You don't need to be a genius

Great entrepreneurs and business owners often seem as though they are amazing geniuses. This just isn't the case. In fact, I have never heard a successful entrepreneur call themselves a genius.

You do not need a degree to build a successful business. One of the benefits of building your own business is that you don't need any qualifications to show how credible you are. I got pretty average GCSE grades, one of which was an E in mathematics, but in my property business I deal with hundreds of thousands of pounds in property investing and development, completing on complex deals that require substantial accuracy. Did I let that stop me from creating my own business?

Sir Richard Branson dropped out of school at the age of sixteen and still managed to build one of the greatest business empires on the planet, Virgin. Forbes estimated his net worth at the time I was writing this book at $5 billion.

David Karp dropped out of school at the age of fifteen. While living in his mother's apartment, he developed the social media and blog site Tumblr. David's net worth according to forbes.com exceeds over $200 million.

Walt Disney dropped out of school at the age of sixteen in the hope of joining the army, but was rejected due to being underage. He then opened up an animations studio with his brother Roy. At the time of his death in 1966, Walt Disney was estimated to be worth $5 billion.

Amancio Ortega didn't even get the chance to attend high school. At the age of fourteen, he moved with his parents to A Coruña, got a job making clothes, and founded ladies' fashion chain Zara. Amancio is worth $74.1 billion.

The examples above show that it's possible to build a successful business without any academic qualifications.

Entrepreneurship isn't a lonely journey

Building a successful business is far from being a lonely pastime. The reason for my success isn't down to some 'special' ability; it's down to the people I decide to work with – my investors, my joint venture partners, my accountant, my videographer, my website developer, my branding consultant, my partner Claire, my book publisher, and my mentors, whose programmes ensure that my chances of succeeding are dramatically increased.

If you set out to achieve business success on your own, you are more likely to fail and quit. You need support, clarity, structure and the right environment. Surround yourself with people who are on the same mission as you and learn from mentors who have vast experience in the areas that you want to succeed in. This will not only save you time, increase your chances of succeeding and reassure you, but it will also make the whole process on the way to the top a lot more fun. If you try to be proficient in all areas of your business, you will miss a lot of opportunity and waste precious time. There is a high possibility that someone has already done what you want to do in business, so there is already a roadmap for you to follow.

When I decided to go into business in the property industry, I knew I had to learn about property, so I decided to surround myself with people whom I could learn from. There is a huge network of entrepreneurs who understand the struggles and frustrations of getting to your desired goal, and many of those entrepreneurs are willing to help. Successful people love helping other people succeed. There are some amazing programmes out there to help you get from point A to point B. From running my property business to my business training company for police officers, I have always joined programmes to help me broaden my way of thinking, hold me to account so I take much more action, bounce ideas off other people and learn today's best practices. It's important to keep up to date with new technologies, legislation and methods.

I have never felt lonely as entrepreneur, and I'm sure you won't either. Reach out to people who can help you.

You don't need lots of cash to start your business

Another myth around building a business is the idea that you need lots of money to get started. There is a term in business called 'bootstrapping', which means to start up a business with limited financial resources. When you bootstrap, you become creative by nature and will find yourself coming up with different ways to gain momentum, which then leads to you being resourceful.

'*Creativity, decisiveness, passion, honesty, sincerity and love. These are the ultimate human resources and when you engage in these resources, you can get any other resource on earth.*'

Tony Robbins

Resourcefulness is the *ultimate* resource. When I made the decision to build a business in 2014, I realised that the best possible chance for me to succeed in doing so would be to surround myself with like-minded people who were on the same 'mission' as me.

A quote from a close friend, Simon Platt, who is also my joint venture partner, comes to mind. He told me when we got our first deal accepted, 'If you can get something from nothing, what can you get from something?' My eyes started to water and I ran into the back room so as not to be seen crying by detainees and other police staff. The quote resonated with me so much, because it made me realise this was only the beginning. My life could have many positive outcomes now I had proved myself capable of gaining results with limited resources.

If you are a police officer thinking that you need lots of money to build your own business, think again. Here are some examples of UK entrepreneurs who started their companies with few financial resources.

Sir Richard Branson started off creating a student magazine at sixteen years old with just £300. According to Forbes, his estimated net worth is now £5 billion.

Peter Hargreaves started off an investment broker business with just £500, working with his business partner from a spare bedroom. According to Forbes, he now has an estimated net worth of £2.8 billion.

J.K. Rowling wrote *Harry Potter and the Philosopher's Stone* in 1995 while living on benefits as a single mother. According to Forbes, her estimated net worth is now £650 million.

If you want to become a successful entrepreneur, one of the most important things you can do is to start. Start with your current resources, and bit by bit you will piece together your own future. Entrepreneurs don't predict their future, they create it.

You don't need to know everything about business to get started

I was caught in a trap, consuming all the content I could find related to business, entrepreneurship, wealth creation and mindset. I would watch hours upon hours of YouTube videos, read book after book, trawl through business forums and network with hundreds of people, always seeking out everything I needed to know when starting a business.

Of course, there are correct ways to start a business, which can save you time, money and energy. However, what I have come to learn over the years is that the best way to learn about business is to be in business, because whatever you know now will soon expand when you start doing things within your own business.

You may get thoughts such as *Yeah, but what if this happens?* or *I don't know how to do that yet, so I can't do this.* Guess what – those thoughts will never cease. I get them and other entrepreneurs get them. We are in a constant state of growth and learning, so we will never know everything there is to know about business.

If you don't know everything, that is a good thing. Imagine a life where you already know every twist and turn, every up and down, and all the people you're going to meet. To me, that seems pretty boring. Besides, there would be no state of growth.

I remember when I was working in custody, the same old people would get arrested at least once or twice a month. They even used to make jokes such as, 'Take me to my en-suite bedroom'. We'd know exactly what they'd been up to, having dealt with them week after week, and this could get pretty mundane. So just because you don't know as much about running a business as you do about being a police officer, don't let it stop you from becoming an entrepreneur. Entrepreneurship isn't about knowing all the answers. In fact, typically entrepreneurs surround themselves with people through their network who do know the answers to the questions they are asking.

I highly recommend you just take the first step, and then the next and the next, and so on. Piece by piece, your knowledge of your business will expand and you will feel confident that you know exactly how things work. Remember, there will always be something new to learn around the corner.

You don't have to be an extrovert to run a business

Some people think that because they are an introvert, they can't be successful. Believe it or not, there are some mega-successful billionaire entrepreneurs who are introverts, such as Mark Zuckerberg (Facebook), Warren Buffett (Berkshire Hathaway), Larry Page (Google), Elon Musk (Tesla and SpaceX) and Bill Gates (Microsoft).

You do not need to be particularly outgoing to achieve success, but you do need to get to work and take action. Talking on the phone, networking, filming on camera and sales are all very learnable skillsets. If you believe you are an introvert, it doesn't matter. You too can achieve an incredible amount of success.

Summary

The six myths we've covered in this chapter are just that – myths. Some are created within our own minds, and some are created by people who either have no business experience or have failed. The reason certain people fail has nothing to do with these myths, and everything to do with their own effort and mindset.

In the next chapter, I want to go into the problems you may be facing in your current role as a police officer.

Chapter 3

Police Officer Problems: Handcuffed to the Job

'Choose a job you love, and you will never have to work a day in your life.'

Confucius

Key learning points:

- You are not alone
- The three biggest issues for police officers around their roles
- Mindset traps

When I was working as a detention officer, I knew the natural progression for me was to become a regular police officer. It was all I'd ever wanted to do. In fact, I had applied when I was eighteen years old and had failed...horribly. When I looked back at that application later in life, I cringed at what

I'd put. I even had affirmations around my bed, stating, 'I will become a police officer by 2015.' (I was massively into Law of Attraction back then). Unfortunately, when I joined custody there had just been a recruitment drive, so I'd missed that opportunity. I was determined that the next time the doors opened, I would be one of the many applying.

However, something strange happened while I was working as a detention officer.

You are not alone

I spoke to many police officers throughout my shifts, helping them with non-compliant detainees, the system we used in custody, booking police interviews, calling solicitors, and of course, engaging in witty banter. But there was one thing I couldn't help with and that was their loss of love for their jobs. The majority of police officers that I became friends with felt overworked, overstretched, tired, lethargic, frustrated, deflated and bored.

I thought, 'What the hell is going on? What is wrong with these officers?'

When I asked my colleagues if they liked their jobs, to my shock, I got replies such as, 'It pays the bills', 'It's not what it used to be', 'It's all right', or a straight no. Not one police officer said they loved the job, or even said anything particularly positive about it. In fact, it became like a little game for me in the end, looking for one positive comment. Now I am sure there are officers who do love the job, but the ones I asked didn't, and I asked quite a few.

I was curious to find out how ex-superintendent Kul Mahay, who achieved his highest rank as temporary chief superintendent, thought about his time in the service.

I thought long and hard for five years, gaining clarity on what I wanted to do to leave the right legacy in the world. My focus had shifted to a much bigger goal. The police service (as passionate as I am about it) has gone through the toughest ten years that I have known. Austerity measures imposed by the government were seeing an excellent service being eroded year after year. I saw frustration, disenchantment and fear expressed on my colleagues' faces more and more. The service that we provided to the public was becoming less compared to its previously high quality.

I knew that if I did not leave two things could happen. Either the job would consume me and lead to stress or poor health, or I would never be able to fulfil my dreams of changing the wider world.

Kul now has a global network of successful and positive people. Since retiring from the service, he has improved his lifestyle significantly by running his own business helping successful leaders and business owners become extraordinary through his unique brand of intensive coaching and immersion training. This is Kul's legacy to the world. His personal relationships are much healthier, he has an incredible amount of freedom to do things he enjoys, he is a healthier human being, he sleeps better, and his mindset has grown stronger. He even gets told he looks younger.

As my time went on as a detention officer, finally the doors opened to accept internal applications for a regular police officer position. This was an extremely exciting time as my chances of becoming a police officer were significantly higher than when I'd applied at the age of eighteen. My time was finally here.

I remember the day vividly. I had printed out the application, my black pen was at the ready and I was about to start filling it in. But my gut wasn't pulling me to complete the application. I asked myself, 'Will I end up feeling the same way as my police officer colleagues feel towards the job? Will I resent my decision to become a police officer? Will I become unhappy?'

To my horror, and eventually my delight, the answer was yes. In that moment, I threw the application in the bin and decided an alternative path would make me happier.

Thankfully that decision paid off as I built my own business.

The three biggest issues for police officers around their roles

Shifts to Success, my business training company, helps support police officers to build successful businesses. When building this business, as well as speaking to police officers from around the UK, I also looked into data conducted by the Police Federation and came across some horrendous findings.

A survey in 2016 of over 43,000 police officers reported that a whopping 55.9% said that their morale was low, and

84.2% stated that this poor morale was due to how the police were treated as a whole. There is a massive problem, and now I knew why I'd had an 'off' feeling in my gut.

Here are the three main problems those police officers had within their role. Maybe you will relate to these problems.

1. A lack of time. Many police officers work long, unsocial shifts which are often extended due to the nature of the job. This takes away precious time with their family and loved ones, as well as time to live their lives as they would like. Of the police officers who took the survey, 58.2% stated that their uneven work-life balance was having a negative effect on their morale.

> Ex-police officer turned-successful-entrepreneur Dionne Buckingham-Brown dealt with two failed marriages because of the amount of time she was spending on shift. Her two children never saw their mother and one ex-husband used to tell her how 'shit' she was because she was never there for the children.
>
> Thankfully, Dionne now has her time back as the owner of Social Sales Academy UK. This company helps other business owners to target their ideal niche and produce more sales through social selling.

Many officers are sacrificing their personal lives for their jobs, but life should not have to be this way.

2. Feeling undervalued. I used to open my pay packet every month and feel undervalued and under-appreciated. Sometimes, my wages didn't seem to add up to the hours I'd actually worked, and I felt so frustrated knowing that I would have to give up even more of my time to rectify this.

Of the police officers who took the 2016 Police Federation Survey, 49.9% agreed that opportunities for development and promotion were severely limited. A whopping 70.9% stated that their pay and benefits, including their pension, were having a negative impact on their morale, and 67.3% stated they didn't feel valued in the police.

> Ex-police officer turned entrepreneur Steven Thompson, who is the founder of BIGDaddy PR, used to work up to ninety hours per week within the service, yet every time he opened his wage slip, the number that he read wasn't pleasing. He knew deep down that he was worth more than the wage he was getting and believed he could earn his true value as an entrepreneur without working as many hours as he did in the police service.
>
> Thankfully, he was right.
>
> He explained to me that the police service assisted in ruining his first marriage, but he had the hindsight to deal with his current relationship in a more positive way, away from the job.

3. **Health and wellbeing.** Police officers deal with dangerous, horrific and stressful situations on a regular basis. I had to do some things I wouldn't wish on anyone while on duty in the police service. I have witnessed a young man with mental health issues rip his nipples clean off then squeeze fatty tissue across the custody cell. I have witnessed people trying to kill themselves and violently self-harm in the cells. And I know

there are many police officers who have seen a lot worse. Over the years, this will have had a negative impact on their mental health.

When speaking to ex-police officer Dionne Buckingham-Brown, who served in the police for twenty-two years, I asked her if she remembered any particularly stressful situations.

Absolutely! I don't mind saying that I had a nervous break-down before taking seven months off on sick leave prior to finally walking out.

I worked as part of a niche department, which was very full on at times. The supervisor we initially had admitted to me that he didn't know what he was doing and was winging it. There were five including him on my team, and he sent one officer away on a long-term course. That person's work was intensive, but I needed it so I could complete my case files as it proved to be an integral part of the cases.

Long story short, the mismanagement of this whole process led me to taking on this other work just so I could get mine done. I was doing the work of four people effectively, with very little support. I asked for help, but I was told to keep on smiling as I was great at my job and everything would be okay.

In the end, I couldn't concentrate. My work suffered greatly and my team effectively turned on me because I couldn't communicate to them exactly how I was feeling. I became a frazzled shell and so much less than the person I had once been.

Once that work was over, we got a new supervisor whom I asked for support and amended working hours. In a nutshell,

I was told that I couldn't reduce my hours, but could work condensed hours. However, a new team member was allowed to reduce her hours, long after I had made the request. When I questioned this, the supervisor didn't like it and our working relationship became fractious. I felt victimised, and there was certainly a lot of passive bullying going on from my immediate supervisor and team mates, which was in fact noticed by other office staff. This led to me developing a long-term stress-related illnesses. I walked out in December 2014 when I had yet another period of sickness, and returned to be told that I would be having my self-certification privileges revoked. I told my supervisor to 'F' off and walked out on sick leave.

I got better and moved departments, hoping for a change. The hours were less stressful, but everyone was so low and demoralised. I decided it was now or never and arranged to take my twenty-eight day notice period as annual leave with HR. I then sent an email to my Inspector, thanked my new office colleagues for welcoming me, and walked out for good. I really couldn't wait to get out that door and become free.

After two years of recovery from chronic fatigue, adrenal stress, migraines, low mood, bad mood, anger rages, depression and even brain scans, Dionne's health is much better now.

It was the best decision I made, to leave the force, especially now my health is much better. It's just not worth risking your health for.

Dionne's example is just one of the many stories I have come across about the stress police officers face. The stress is compounded by an anxious worrying feeling that some day your decisions as a police officer may come back to haunt you. Figures from the Police Federation show a huge 52% of police officers saying that workload and responsibilities are having a negative effect on morale. According to the Office of National Statistics, from 2001–2013 a total of 248 police officers took their own lives. Many police officers feel as though they have a lack of support from the organisation.

PC Rob Webber, who is a serving police officer, founded a charity called Call4Backup. The charity is to support police officers, staff and volunteers to find a solution to any strains that might be impacting on their lives with the mission of making their work and home lives more manageable. A colleague who has been there and knows the unique role the police service plays provides initial crisis intervention, followed by signposting via support lines. The charity then offers ongoing support and, in certain circumstances, counselling.

When I spoke to Rob, he explained that his charity is different from others as it is a peer support charity that was founded by police officers for those in the police service.

The charity has been independent from all police services from the outset as there is a lot of distrust in the police service, and this can inhibit employees from reaching out and seeking wellbeing support. We are confidential and independent, and we hope that this increases trust and encourages those who may not reach out to reconsider.

I asked Rob why he set up the charity.

In 2015, I personally lost a friend to severe depression. At the time he took his life, he was on the other side of the country and I just wish he had called me. I knew of many other officers who had been through issues with their mental health and felt that there was a need for better support from and for colleagues.

After hearing this, I asked Rob why he believed more and more officers were developing PTSD (post-traumatic stress disorder) and depression.

The pressures on individual officers have increased over the last few years and this is largely down to austerity. The cuts in police numbers have meant that those left in the force will find themselves having to do a lot more with the same amount of time. This constant pressure results in the stresses being too hard to manage. Once this is coupled with an incident where there is some personal connection, a person may not have the resilience to deal with the stresses and this is what causes mental health issues to develop.

To put austerity into context, the police forces in the UK have lost over 20,000 officers since 2010. Practically, this is more than the 16,000 officers who were called into London to deal with the August riots and disorder of 2011. This doesn't take into consideration the loss of civilian posts, meaning those officers and staff left are now doing more than they can mentally cope with.'

If you know anyone who may benefit from Rob's charity Call4Backup, you can contact him on 08445 899957 or info@call4backup.org, or check out his charity's website at: www.call4backup.org.

The reality of these problems is that police officers feel institutionalised and 'handcuffed' to the job, believing this is as good as it gets, which creates inertia. It begs the question, 'Why don't police officers just get another job?' and I asked myself that exact question.

PC Anna James (not her real name), a close friend and serving police officer, wanted a better life with more time and income and less stress. She was fed up with feeling undervalued despite constantly facing risky situations, and because of this applied to become a supermarket manager. She got the job and was over the moon, but as soon as she stepped into the corporate world, things didn't go so well for her.

She missed her identity as a police officer. It was all that she had ever known. So after four months working in the supermarket, she actually reapplied to the police service to become an officer again. However, now she is back on duty, dealing with the same issues and frustrations and feeling as though she is back to square one.

I took a risk to have a better life in another job, but I soon realised this wasn't going to be the case. I am glad I took that risk as now I know working for someone else isn't the route to go. But I am still frustrated with the lack of resources within the police service. I am not being 'allowed' annual leave and I am working so much overtime. I am physically exhausted, and in some instances I am not able to eat or drink during my entire shift.

I am now looking at starting my own business as an entrepreneur, creating my own team while keeping my identity without being dictated to by policy in another job role.

Even if police officers get another job away from the police service, their lives will still be dictated by policy. They are trading one job for another. With their own business as an entrepreneur, they are not. In fact, on my business programme, I help ensure that police officers are not creating another job for themselves by teaching them how to set up the correct systems. They are in control 100%.

Mindset traps

Working overtime. I see police officers make this mistake all the time. To earn more income, they trade more of their time. The problem with this is that they spend more time away from family and loved ones and the things they enjoy doing, and end up taking on more stress. This mindset leads to a dead end, plus due to the higher tax threshold, officers find themselves working harder and longer with less pay off.

The pension. When I was working in the police service, the pension always seemed to come up in conversation. Police officers would talk about how their pensions had changed and if they were in the new scheme or old scheme. They would tell each other how long they had until they retired.

Thinking in this way will keep them handcuffed to the job until the day they do retire. Police officers who are focused on their pensions are missing out on amazing earning potential as business owners. Besides, if they do decide to start their own business, it doesn't mean they lose their police pension.

I would always advise police officers to start building a

business while they are still serving. This way, the transition from employee to entrepreneur is much smoother, and once you do transition to full-time business owner, you can place a percentage of your newfound profit into a better pension or high yielding investment.

The sad truth about pensions is that you can only get access to them when you retire. Do you really want to wait that long to enjoy money and the freedom it brings?

One of ex-superintendent turned successful entrepreneur Kul Mahay's biggest frustrations was when he spoke to colleagues coming up to retirement and they had no future plans.

When I asked officers what their plans were after retirement from the force, they would simply look blankly at me and say they had no idea, or they were keeping their options open, or they'd just rest after having worked hard for thirty years. While I am not telling everyone to start their own business, it is vital, for your own continued health, to focus on something going forward. Don't become old way before your time.

Police officers are relatively young when they retire, and yet so many adopt the 'retired' mentality and consequently end up experiencing all the ailments that older people experience. Stay active in your mind, not just your body. Focus on what dreams you have left unfulfilled and make them come true. Which being in business can surely help you achieve.

Ex-police officer Dionne Buckingham-Brown, who is the co-founder of Social Sales Academy UK, realised this.

> *A few years prior to leaving the police force, I had huge worries about the effect it would have on my pension contributions in that I feared I had paid too much in to leave. The pension reform proposals actually made it easier for me to overcome this thought process. I then froze my pension at seventeen years' service which took me out of the 'pension trap' mindset.*
>
> *By the time I actually left the police force, I didn't have many concerns. I knew that despite being a single mother, having a mortgage and other financial commitments, I would make enough money from my business as an entrepreneur to support myself and my family.*

Dionne has an excellent point: the pension can be a mindset trap if you let it. Knowing that you can far out-earn whatever your pension will be is a strong reason not to let it trap you, especially with the new pension reform. Also ask yourself, do you trust the government not to change your pension further down the line? From my research many police officers don't. You should chase your passion, not your pension.

Rest days. Police officers work long, unsociable hours, feeling tired and overworked. If you don't want to carry on feeling like this until you are in your fifties, you need to change your thinking about your rest days. Start using them to your advantage.

When I was working twelve-hour shifts in custody, I used to get four rest days for every four days on duty. I called these my 'Success Days'. Every Success Day, I ensured that I devoted my time and effort to high-priority tasks that would move my business forward. Eventually, my business and life success developed.

I understand that you may have many things you want to do on your rest days. However, by repeating the same pattern, you will remain in the job for many years to come, continuing to work long, unsociable shifts away from your family and deal with copious amounts of stress. If you put in the work on your very own Success Days, you will create the opportunity to transition into being a full-time entrepreneur. All those rest days you sacrificed will be worth it, as then you will gain back the working hours to put into your life the way you want to.

Relying on the government to make change. Waiting for the government to make changes to police organisations, whether that is more funding for police officers to join the service or a pay rise for the hard work you put in during your shift, is not something you should hold your breath for. This lets someone else take control of your life, and can keep you waiting for years.

The data from the Home Office on Police Workforce, England and Wales, 30 September 2016, suggest further decreases for police worker types. Nationally, the volumes of workforce and changes since 30 September 2015 were:

- 122,859 police officers, a decrease of 2.2%
- 60,815 police staff, a decrease of 3.1%
- 10,551 PCSOs (police community support officers), a decrease of 10.7%
- 3,990 designated officers, a decrease of 5.9%
- 14,864 special constables, a decrease of 7.3%

The decreases have been happening since 2010, and it doesn't look as though anything is going to change soon. These decreases are one of the main causes of the problems that police officers face: a lack of time, a lack of income and heaps of stress.

Instead of waiting for the government to make positive changes, take personal responsibility for your life and take action, because no one is going to help you but you.

Summary

In this chapter, we have learnt in depth what other police officers from around the UK are feeling. There are common mindset traps that lead police officers to keep on following the same actions that ultimately keep them 'handcuffed' to the job. If we think like the majority, we will end up like the majority.

Data from the Police Federation Survey suggest that 61% of police officers have a lack of options to consider when leaving the police service. Hoping is not an effective strategy; acting is.

In Part 2, we will look in detail at my Business Builder Model, highlighting the options for police officers through the exciting journey as an entrepreneur. It all starts with an idea.

PART 2

How To Build A Successful Business

Chapter 4

Ideas

'The clash of ideas is the sound of freedom.'

Lady Bird Johnson

Key learning points:

- Different business industries
- Different ways to generate business ideas
- How to validate your business ideas
- Market research
- Your unique selling proposition
- How to niche your business idea

Every great business began with an idea, and this is why 'ideas' is the first step in my six-step Business Builder Model. The model is a natural progression that successful businesses take, so be sure not to skip ahead. Lean in to the process and enjoy the exciting entrepreneurial journey ahead.

Different business industries

There is a common myth that all good ideas have been taken which is, to be honest, completely irrelevant. People were already using mobile phones when Steve Jobs, co-Founder of Apple, decided to invent the iPhone. Social media platforms were already about when Mark Zuckerberg co-founded Facebook, and there was already a running shoe when Phil Knight created Nike. Just because someone is already doing your idea, there's no reason why you shouldn't bring that idea to fruition for yourself.

There are many different industries that you can get involved in. I highly recommend you Google different business industries to broaden your thinking. See what you may be interested in, and remember you don't have to be passionate about something to succeed in it. Just find something that piques your interest.

Here are a few examples of different industries to get you started:

- Arts
- Computers
- Education
- Health
- Financial
- Kids and teens
- Business
- Personal development
- Games
- Home
- Recreation

- Shopping
- Sports

Within these industries are different sub-categories. For example, my company Shifts to Success would fall under Education, but as a sub-category it would fall under Business because I am teaching business methods and strategies to police officers. The company My Protein would fall under Health, but as a sub-category it would fall under Supplements or Nutrition. Within each industry you come across, you can always go deeper to be more specific. You can also combine them as entrepreneurship can be multi-dimensional.

Different ways to generate business ideas

'Ideas are cheap. Ideas are easy. Ideas are common. Everyone has ideas. Ideas are highly, highly overvalued. Execution is all that matters.'

Casey Neistat, entrepreneur, YouTube
personality, filmmaker and vlogger

And he is perfectly right. Believe it or not, coming up with business ideas is the easy part. It only took ex-police officer Dionne two months to go from idea to sustainable business, producing a monthly income of £6,500. How? She took action on her idea and didn't quit just because someone else was using the same idea already. All great entrepreneurs have developed the habit of taking action on their ideas, which we will go into later in the book.

However, not all of us do come up with ideas. Now I want

to share with you ten different ways to come up with business ideas so you can start taking action on them.

1. Do something about what pisses you off. Founder and CEO of Klickly, Cooper Harris, was inspired by frustration when she came up with her idea. She wanted to donate money to a charity through a link when she was scrolling through her social media, but found that the whole process was too complicated and she had to go through several steps. Thus her tech company Klickly was founded.

When a guy call Colin Barceloux was in college in America, he thought textbooks cost far too much. So, in 2007, two years after graduating, he decided to take action and founded BookRenter.com, a California-based business that offers textbook rentals at about a 60% discount. What began as a solo operation created out of frustration now has 1.5 million users and 200 employees.

'You just have to look at what frustrates you,' he says. 'There's your business idea right there.'

2. Look for new niches. In the next chapter, we will go into more depth about niches. However, coming up with a niche is a great way to generate a business idea. Your business idea doesn't have to reinvent the wheel. Take a look at what some of the big players in an industry are missing and figure out if you can fill the gaps.

In 2003, Stephen Key started the company HotPicks, now based in California, after realising the major brands in the guitar plectrum industry wasn't offering collectible novelty plectrums. So he designed a skull-shaped plectrum that filled an empty niche and was soon sold in 1,000 stores. This in turn helped him achieve financial independence.

He said, 'The big guys leave a tremendous amount of opportunity on the table. All you need to do is look for it,' which I think is pretty cool.

3. Talk to shoppers. There's no better way to come up with an idea that meets people's needs than to talk to shoppers. If you are interested in mountain bikes, for example, go to sports and bike shops and ask customers what they wish they could find in the marketplace. If you're interested in developing an e-commerce business (online store business), consider sending an online survey to potential customers to learn about their needs and interests. The feedback you get from your potential market is extremely valuable because then you can plan a business where there is a demand for it.

4. Play the mix and match game. Walk up and down the aisles of supermarkets, electric appliance shops or toy stores, combining two products across the aisle from each other into one. That should spark quite a few ideas, but be prepared for most of them to be bad. Every once in a while, though, you will find a brilliant idea.

5. Solve a problem. Entrepreneurs solve a problem that the market has. Look for problems or tasks around your home or workplace that could potentially be made easier by a new product or service. If you identify an issue that someone else hasn't already solved, chances are there will be a market for it. However, if it has already been thought of, don't worry. There may be potential for you to make it better.

Also, listen to your colleagues, friends and family when they complain, because the thing they are complaining about could be solved through your entrepreneurial idea.

6. Apply your skills to an entirely new field. Think about your skills and whether they might be useful in a new area. Ask yourself what you are good at, and believe me, you *are* good at something.

For example, I used to hold investor days where I would teach newbie investors how to build and manage a property business. I loved doing this and it gave me a real buzz. The feedback I got from each trainee was so positive that I knew I had a skill in teaching others in an interactive way. I am now applying this skillset into my other company, Shifts to Success, which is a new field in teaching business methods and principles.

Ex-superintendent Kul Mahay is now the Founder of Kul Mahay International Ltd. He explains how he used his skillset in a new field.

Having spent a third of my adult life in senior leadership positions, I recognise the unique pressures that leaders undergo. How the job or the position can consume you. While the outside world sees your position, status, relative wealth and labels you as 'successful', very few remember that you are also human, with all the imperfections and pressures of being a human being. In fact, many senior leaders and business owners feel lonely and disconnected. It affects their health and relationships. It certainly did for me.

I now help others in the same position to reconnect with themselves and master the art of inner leadership to become outstanding in all areas of their lives.

7. Find a category lacking recent innovations. Another great way to generate business ideas is to look at markets that haven't had many recent innovations. When I started lifting weights in 2011, I also stated to consume protein shakes and bought myself a couple of shakers. These allowed me to mix up my shake to ensure there weren't any clumpy bits. The shakers did the job, but as time went on, I noticed that the market changed considerably. Entrepreneurs developed new features for protein shakers, from a classic shaker with a metal mixer ball inside to shakers that had different compartments in them to hold other supplements such as vitamins tablets. Then companies introduced battery-powered shakers, with a mini plastic mixer at the bottom to whisk the protein supplement at the push of a button.

What market do you believe needs innovating?

8. Make a cheaper version of an existing product. When entrepreneur Michael Dubin founded the Dollar Shave Club, a subscription-based grooming brand in the US, he started by undercutting big competitors in his industry. His company grew at a phenomenally fast rate, and within five years, Michael sold it for a reported one billion dollars to Unilever.

9. Let go of originality. There are countless businesses already in existence, so it's likely that you won't be the first person to think of an idea or product. Focus on how to be better, rather than how to be different. Make a list of businesses that you find inspiring or align well with your values, then ask yourself how you could put your own stamp on that product or industry. This thinking will get your juices flowing.

10. **Change your routine.** When you stretch your thinking, seek out things that you would normally miss. Change your fixed routine by listening to podcasts, watching inspiring business and entrepreneurial interviews on YouTube and engaging in conversations that talk about the future. Break the mould you currently find yourself in. When you do this, your vision gets much wider and business ideas will pour in.

So now we have gone through ten ways to generate business ideas, the next step is to see if your business idea is good enough to start working on.

How to validate your business ideas

How do you know if you have a business idea worth pursuing? You don't want to waste time in its development if it isn't, but you will not know if your business idea is worth developing until you implement it and move forward. You can, however, feel more confident that you can turn your idea into fully-fledged business by asking yourself three questions to stretch your thinking.

1. **Is there competition?** You want competition for your business idea. If you find a market that is 100% unoccupied, you're either the first one there, which is a tad risky as there is no roadmap to follow, or people have tried out the idea and abandoned it because they have been unsuccessful.

By having competition, you can look at other business models and see how things work.

2. **Are my competitors making money?** You need to make sure your competitors are making the kind of money you want

to make. Look on their websites for testimonials and client success stories. Ask them – give them a call; ask about their fees, rates or packages. Try not to tell them why you are doing this research, though, as they will believe they are giving away all their business secrets.

A great question to ask is, 'How many people have actually used your service/product as I want to make sure it works?' This gives you an approximate number of units they have sold, which you multiply by the cost of the product/service. By doing this, you will get a general sense of how your competitors are doing and how much money they are earning.

3. Can I offer my competitors' product/service/idea differently and/or better? If you show you are unique, you will attract the kind of customers who will buy from you time and time again and refer you to other potential customers.

The point of difference between you and your competition is your unique selling proposition (USP). For example, is your price cheaper? Is your design better? Is your way of delivering the product better? Does your product produce better results? Can you provide more value? Etc. There are many ways to deliver your USP.

By answering yes to these three questions, you are off to a great start in developing that idea. The next step of developing your business idea is to conduct market research.

Market research

Conducting proper due diligence via market research is crucial when you decide to take the entrepreneurial journey, but often people neglect this process because they don't want to hear any negative feedback.

Failing to conduct market research can take a company to an early grave, and companies that do perform proper market research are often the ones that succeed. But what does market research actually mean? Here's how the Entrepreneur.com website defines it.

> 'The process of gathering, analysing and interpreting information about a market, about a product or service to be offered for sale in that market, and about the past, present and potential customers for the product or service; research into the characteristics, spending habits, location and needs of your business's target market, the industry as a whole, and the particular competitors you face.'

When we break down that definition, we find some key points:

- Products or services
- Past, present and potential customers
- Customer characteristics
- Spending habits
- Location
- Needs of customers
- Research into the market industry (what are others doing)
- Competition

Examine each of the key areas highlighted above by collecting data from two different types of market research, primary and secondary.

Primary research. The objective of primary research is to collect data, either yourself or by hiring someone, directly from the source, which will be your customers or potential customers. I would advise doing it yourself at the early stages of developing your business because then you will get a real feel for your customers' or potential customers' problems. Send them surveys, questionnaires, feedback forms and scorecard quizzes.

You can see an example of a quiz at www.shiftstosuccess.com.

Once you have all this data, you can then formalise it.

Secondary research. The objective of secondary research is to collect data that has already been formalised for your business industry and market. This can be found on competitors' websites, forums, in reports, books and other available content. Secondary research is especially useful at the early stages of your entrepreneurial journey when you don't have many customers.

When you look at the data from your market research efforts, you will see what problems your potential customers have. What are their frustrations? How can you best solve their problems? What barriers will they have in buying your product? What demographics are they (male or female, in their twenties or forties, etc.)? What do they normally buy and from whom? Where do your customers originate from? What are your competitors offering them and how can you offer something better?

There is a ton of valuable data at your fingertips, and when you have this data you can better prepare yourself to build a business that has a higher chance of succeeding because you understand your customers and your competitors.

When I conducted market research on police officers, I posted a survey on a Facebook forum. Within two days, I had over 100 pieces of valuable data around the problems they were facing within the job, why they hadn't decided to leave and why they hadn't started their own businesses. I also spoke directly to police officers, either by phone or face to face. By collecting all this data, I could fully understand police officers' problems and plan how to solve them. It also gave me content ideas so that I could work towards developing a product.

This is an example of primary market research.

Another thing I did was look online to see what data organisations such as the Police Federation, the Home Office and police forums had already collected which aligned well with my primary research. This confirmed that I was on the right tracks and gave me confidence to go forward with creating my business and developing products.

This is an example of secondary market research.

Now we have covered market research and what type of data to collect, I now want to help you discover what your unique selling proposition (USP) will be.

Your unique selling proposition

Nine times out of ten, after conducting market research, you will have discovered that someone else is already doing your idea. Remember, this is a good thing. But you do need to differentiate yourself from your competition, otherwise your potential customers will remain their customers.

That is one big reason why it's so important to find

your USP, but what are the other reasons for finding it? And how do you find your USP in the first place? Let's get into it.

There is a load of information out there, and your customers are likely to research before buying a product or service. If you cannot separate yourself from your competition, you are in fact creating more competition for yourself, which will ultimately drive down sales. Even worse, it could link your business to a competitor who has a bad reputation.

Having a USP is also important as you will feel more confident that you can deliver on a promise and your potential customers won't look elsewhere. A USP identifies a clear direction for your business and develops your business's personality. This helps your customers and your chosen business industry to remember your reputation and brand.

So, how do you find your USP? A great place to start is by asking yourself these five questions:

- How is my business better than my competitors'?
- What makes my business outstanding?
- Why will people buy from me?
- What are my special talents or skills?
- What makes my product or service superior?

Ensure that you write down all the answers to these questions so as not to forget them. Often the answers will spur on your creative mindset and you will think of various ways to come up with your USP. It's important that your USP conveys a benefit to your customer, such as a promise, guarantee, performance standard or an area of excellence.

Another way to find your USP is to look at your market research. Pick out your competitors and go online to find complaints or bad reviews from their customers. From these complaints, pick out what your business can offer that your competitors are failing at. Just remember that you have to deliver on your USP's promise.

Finding a niche, need or gap in the market is an excellent way of finding your USP. For example, my company, Shifts to Success, only supports police officers or ex-police officers to build successful businesses.

How to niche your business idea

A niche is a targetable part of a market that you can provide a product or service to that focuses on a specific market need. If you niche your business idea, you can put forward much more detail in your products or services than if you were to offer them to the general market. A niche is less about what you do and more about whom you serve.

People like to work with people who know, like and understand them and their unique problems. For example, my niche is police officers. Even though my company is a business training company that could serve others in various markets, I decided to work with police officers, because I understand their problems and really want to make a difference in transforming their lives. Ex-superintendent Kul Mahay's business industry is leadership coaching, which could be executed across serval markets. However, he has niched down his market to senior and successful leaders and business owners.

Having a niche is important as you know whom to focus your marketing efforts on. The more you work with your niche market, the more you become known, which then results in customers seeking you out. If your marketing efforts try and capture the attention of everyone in a business industry, you may not grab the attention of anyone, which of course doesn't lead to profitable sales.

It is also important to ensure you narrow your niche down. For example, offering your fitness advice to women isn't niche enough. However, offering your services to women in the UK over forty who have had children and work full-time with an income of £20,000+ is a niche. Being specific wins.

Here are a few examples of niches:

- If you have an interest in dogs and would like to build a business around it, you could sell products or services to new owners of miniature dachshunds with two or more puppies
- If you have an interest in vegan food, which is pretty niche already, you could sell advice products to women who work in the public sector and have decided to go vegan for the first time
- If you have an interest in sailing, you could sell advice, products or equipment to help male newbies in their fifties sail with confidence and fun
- If you are interested in personal training, you could teach busy mothers how to lose twenty pounds and look sexier

All you have to do is pick a business industry, preferably one that interests you, and then delve deeper into that industry to offer your services or product to a specific market. The possibilities are endless with niches, and if you invest time in finding a niche for your business, it will ultimately save you time, as well as money and energy.

Summary

There are many business industries out there, but just because someone is already doing your idea, don't be put off pursuing it for yourself. In this chapter, we have covered ten different ways to come up with business ideas, and how to validate those business ideas with three simple questions. We have talked about why market research is so important before you build a business, and how to conduct it to collect valuable data within your business industry. Finding your USP is crucial for your businesses success, and finding a market niche for your business is important too.

In the next chapter, I will be going through the second step of my Business Builder Model, Planning.

Success Story – Katie Saywell

Katie Saywell worked for Nottinghamshire police for over ten years as a PC. Wanting to fulfil her potential and lead a better life, she decided to go into business, but had no business idea or previous experience.

Katie joined Shifts to Success, which helped her identify her skill-sets and come up with a business idea. She is now the founder of The Dogs Code, a specialist dachshund training company. Since starting her business, Katie has:

- Established herself as an industry leader
- Gained thousands of followers on social media
- Won a business award from *Dragons Den*'s Theo Paphitis
- Made thousands in sales and gained customers globally
- Resigned from the police force and gone into business full time

When I asked Katie how her life has changed, she explained:

Since joining Shifts to Success, I have a different approach to my working life. It's given me the capability to start my own business with the most amazingly supportive group of individuals and mentors. I created a business from scratch because I believed and trusted in the journey.

The strongest impact for me is personal development – there is so much more to life. I've been given the ability to believe in myself, shifting my mindset to success. Not only that, but my personal confidence has grown tremendously. I am now fully competent in social media marketing, creating videos, doing live streams, speaking to large groups of people and, of course, making sales for my business which help solve my customers' problems.

All of this has allowed me to resign from a full-time job in the police and live life on my terms. I am now free to do what I want and there is no looking back.

Chapter 5

Planning

'Failing to plan is planning to fail.'

Alan Lakein

Key learning points:

- Your business plan
- Legal structure
- Company name
- Domain name and social media
- Personal finances and business bank account
- The Business Model Canvas
- Insurances

Your business plan

Creating a business plan is important when you set off on the entrepreneurial journey to achieve success. It's difficult to arrive at your destination without a map. This map will be your business plan.

Your initial business plan will guide you at the beginning, but it will change over time, and that is an important thing to keep in mind. Just because they're written down doesn't mean your plans can't change. You will come across new insights, new strategies and your goals will widen.

Your business plan should be no longer than one page, and will include everything you need to refer back to each day. You can make a ten-page business plan if you wish, but it will change so often at the beginning, it's not productive to spend time rewriting a lengthy plan. Your one-page business plan can be updated with ease and it provides clarity.

Here are the things to include in your one-page business plan:

TITLE. Give your business plan a name to make it real and tangible. Insert your company name at the top, or simply write 'business plan' if you don't have a name yet.

GOALS. Write down your short-term goals (twelve months), your mid-term goals (one to three years) and long-term goals (three to five years). How much income do you want? How many sales do you want to make? How much content do you want to produce? How many email subscribers do you want? How many people have you reached? What media have you been featured in? Be specific with your goals.

TARGET MARKET. Write down whom you will be marketing and selling to. Be specific. Remember to niche.

HOW MANY CUSTOMERS DO YOU NEED? Write down how many customers you need to make the kind of profit you want.

Include the amount of loyal customers who will buy from you whenever you release a product.

YOUR USP. Write down what makes you different from your competitors. What makes you unique and better?

YOUR BIGGEST THREE COMPETITORS. Write down your top three competitors so you know whom you are constantly trying to be better than/different from.

TEAM. Write down who you will need on your team. Are you outsourcing work to freelancers on www.peopleperhour.com, www.upwork.com, www.freelance.co.uk, www.fiverr.com (videographer, designer, web developer, market researcher, virtual assistant, etc.)?

MARKETING. Write down how you will generate leads (Facebook ads, Google Ads, referrals). How will you attract leads? What is your budget per month for generating leads?

PRODUCTS AND SERVICES. Write down what you will be selling. What will your profit margins be (how much will your products/services sell for and how much will it cost to produce them)?

VALUES. Write down your business values.

MISSION. What is the mission for your business? For example, the mission for my company, Shifts to Success, is to help and support 100 police officers in building successful businesses by 2020, providing them with more income, time and passion.

Congratulations! You now know how to create a map to set off on your exciting entrepreneurial journey. Don't forget to update it when needed and ensure you place it where you'll see and read it every day, such as on the bathroom mirror or next to your bed. It's important to read it every day to ensure you are following the plan.

Next let's learn all about the basic legal structures for setting up your company.

Legal structure

I must declare that I am not an accountant or tax advisor, so please seek professional advice when setting up your company.

Setting up a legal structure is one of the first things you will do when you go into business. There are five main types of company: sole trader, limited company, ordinary business partnership, limited partnership and limited liability partnership, and unincorporated association. The structure you choose will ultimately affect your legal responsibilities, the taxes you will have to pay and how you will take profit from your company. However, I have only highlighted the two structures which I believe will be more practical for police officers who are looking to start their first business.

Sole trader. This is best suited for individuals. As a sole trader, you will have full control of the business and full profit retention.

Sole traders are usually local businesses such as tradespeople. There are some disadvantages to being a sole trader, such as having unlimited liability. This means that if the business goes into debt, you as the business owner are fully responsible and your home, savings, car etc. could be at risk. If you do want to expand in the future, it is more difficult to get funding in this legal set up.

As a sole trader you will need to register with HMRC and file a self-assessment tax return.

Limited company (limited by shares). These are the most common in the UK. In this type of company, the shareholders are liable up to the amount of the shares they have purchased. Directors are not financially liable as long as the law isn't broken.

You can register your limited company at Companies House or by using one of the several online services available. Directors of the company are legally responsible for submitting annual returns, statutory accounts, a company tax return and registering for VAT at the correct point. A good accountant can do these things for you.

Remember, when you're choosing a legal structure it is important to seek professional advice from an accountant. They will advise on a structure that will best suit your company.

Company name

Choosing a company name is just as important as choosing the name of your children, because that's the name your company will be known by for the duration of its life. You don't want your company's name to be linked to anything that might make it look bad, just like you don't see many kids with the name Adolf.

Below are five different things to consider when picking your company name.

1. Aspiration. You can name your business based on your aspiration, in other words your desired outcome for it. This way, you are highlighting your business's benefits in your business name. Your target market will then already have a good idea about what you do before they know anything else about your business. If you do it right, your USP will be clear from your business name, effectively differentiating you from your competitors.

Here are some examples of businesses named after aspirations:

- Loans Approved
- Stick and Click Lights
- Five Hour Energy

2. Problem. This is similar to naming your business based on an aspiration, but instead of focusing on the thing that people want to happen, focus on the thing they don't want to happen – the problem that they're trying to avoid.

The best way to come up with this type of business name is to ask your potential customers, 'What's your biggest problem when it comes to your life? Do you have any frustrations when dealing with companies or people from a certain business industry?' By collecting this data, you can then take their issues and place them into your business name, providing you with a USP.

Here are some examples of businesses that picked the problem method:

- Streak Free Windows
- Never Lost Pet tags
- FatBlaster

3. Alliteration. Pick a 'controlling' word, then go through the dictionary and find a matching word that starts with the same letter. The reason why this makes a good business name is that it's memorable and easy to say.

Here are a few examples:

- Weight Watchers
- Paramount Pictures
- Fitness First

4. Invention. With this method you have to get your creative juices flowing, as you will be coming up with a word that doesn't exist yet. Here are some examples of companies that invented words that everyone seems to know now.

- Avon
- Google
- Ikea
- Lego

Just be mindful that it may take years for your business name to catch on, and in some cases it can cost quite a bit of money for it to become a part of people's everyday life.

5. Word mash. With the word mash method, you also invent a word. However, it's much easier than the invention method because your word comes from mixing parts of two other words together.

Make a list of all your company's features and benefits. Then play mix and match to see which words can be creatively merged.

Here are some examples of businesses that use the word mash method:

- Microsoft – a combination of microcomputer and software
- Wikipedia – a combination of Wiki and encyclopaedia
- FedEx – a combination of federal and express
- Groupon – a combination of group and coupon

Now you have five different ways to come up with your company name, I want to help you avoid common mistakes.

Avoid initials. People will often forget names like AOI Florists or WNC Jewellery

Avoid using your own name. At some point you may want to remove yourself from the business or sell it.

Don't choose a name too similar to your competitor's. This can confuse your potential customers, and just because a name is working for your competitor doesn't necessarily mean it will work for you. Remember to be different – think back to your USP. Also, the company can sue you for infringement of copyright.

Don't choose anything too local. By doing this, you would essentially be restricting yourself from branching out.

Don't choose a name based on a current service. As your business matures and new technologies become available, you will release new services and products. Just because you offer a certain service successfully at present doesn't mean you won't offer different services in the future.

I hope the above helps you when it comes to picking your company name. This process is fun, and it is something that you will build your legacy upon. Bounce the different company names you come up with off your family and colleagues. They might add something creative to this mix.

Domain name and social media

You will also need a domain name for your website. It's important to try and get www.yourcompanyname.com, because .com is the most popular domain. When you have decided on a company name, find out if the domain is available. There is a great website that I use called www.namecheckr.com. This website will save you time and energy in trawling through the internet to find out if your domain and social media names are available. All you need to do is type in the name you want and it will show you what availability there is across social media platforms and domains.

If you find that your business, domain and social media names are all available and you are happy with them, buy them immediately. Do not wait as someone else may take them. Social media is free, so go straight to platforms such as Facebook, Twitter, Instagram, YouTube, etc. and register your name.

To buy your domain, you can go to several online websites to do so, but I have always used www.uk.godaddy.com.

Domains are pretty cheap to buy, and this ensures there won't be any issues or complications in the future with regards to competition or haters. I bought all the domains I could relating to my businesses and my personal name. This way no one can create a website based on them.

The domain names that are the most important and recognised are .com, .co.uk, .net, .global. Remember when you buy these to set them up for auto-renew so that they stay as your domains. If they do not get renewed then they are available to the market once again.

If you are struggling with anything related to domains, call the relevant customer service department. GoDaddy has been very helpful for me in the past.

The next stage is getting your finances in order.

Personal finances and business bank accounts

When you decide to go into business it is always a good thing to prepare your finances for the journey ahead. By doing the little exercise below, you could actually find money you didn't think you had.

Print off your bank statements for the past three months, grab a pen or highlighter and mark each outgoing that you think you could live without. If you have a partner, I recommend you do this exercise together so that you are in agreement. I wouldn't like to cause any domestics.

Now when I say live without, I mean live without. You don't have to be drastic and throw away the TV because you're wasting electricity watching it, but you may discover you can cut back on certain things that you regularly pay for. Then that money can be used towards your business. When I did this exercise with my partner, we found between us magazine subscriptions, online memberships and TV packages we could cancel. We then looked at things we did need but could save money on, changing brands, phone contracts and supermarkets. Overall we saved £297 per month – £3,564 per year.

It may seem like you will be cutting back on a lot of things, but the truth is that you can always go back to these things when you have a successful business that is producing the kind of income you want. All you will be doing is making a short-term sacrifice for a long-term gain. Trust me, it's worth it.

Another part of planning your finances for your business is getting a business bank account. Again, I must declare that I am not a professional financial advisor; I am just sharing my experiences with you.

You do not want to use your everyday bank account as your business account. This is something I did with my first company and it made a mess of things in relation to my book keeping and accounts. Set up a business account using the correct business product from the bank – you can do this with your current bank or choose a new one. So as not to get confused, I went with a new bank. I checked comparison websites and found a certain bank that offered better products for me at that particular time.

Opening a business bank account in the UK is a fairly simple process. In general, you'll only be asked to prove your identity and address, with documents such as:

- Proof of ID for all named company directors – passport, photo driving licence or national ID card
- Proof of address – recent bank statement or utility bill, or council tax statement
- If you're applying from abroad, you may be asked to provide notarised translations of your ID and documents used to prove your address

You'll also need to give details of your company, such as:

- Full business address (including postcode)
- Contact details
- Companies House registration number (for limited companies and partnerships)
- Estimated annual turnover

Don't put off getting your business account sorted because you may be earning income sooner than you think. But to earn money, it is important to understand how business models work.

The Business Model Canvas

The Business Model Canvas was first introduced by entrepreneur, speaker and business model innovator, Alexander Osterwalder, and it is a great way to get thoughts from your head in to something more tangible. With the Business Model Canvas, we will gain clarity on how your business will operate.

The Business Model Canvas has nine different segments. The first five segments are what your customers see and interact with, and how you are capturing value. Segments six to nine are your infrastructure and operations needed to support and run your business.

The different segments are:

1. Customer
2. Value proposition
3. Channels
4. Customer relationships
5. Revenue streams
6. Key resources
7. Activities
8. Partners
9. Costs

1. Customer. You need to define who your customer is. If you have highlighted your niche, that's exactly what this section is for.

For example, your customers could be men over fifty years of age who want to learn how to play polo in the UK.

2. Value proposition. This is what products and services you offer. What solution do you provide to your customers? Think about their problem and how you can offer a product and/or service to solve it.

Also think about your USP and how you differentiate yourself from your competitors. What will make your product, service or business more attractive to your customers?

For example, your product could be a Facebook marketing programme, and your USP could be that if your customers find themselves confused or stuck, you offer free consultations to help them get up and running (customer service).

3. Channels. This is the route to market. How does your product or service get to your customers? Do you deliver your product online? Do you deliver your service on the cloud? Or maybe you deliver it physically.

For example, a product I created called The HMO Success Pack was delivered online. People would enter their bank details and click 'Pay', then download the pack.

4. Customer relationships. This is all about how you will get your customers in the first place, how you will keep them and how you will grow your customer base. In other words, it's about generating leads and using strategies to ensure customers stay loyal and recommend you to others.

For example, banks generate leads by running TV adverts. They then keep their customers by having them set up accounts with attractive benefits. They grow their customer base by offering other products such as loans.

5. Revenue streams. This is how you actually generate money from the value proposition that you offer to your customer segment. What strategies will you be using to capture income from your customers? Will it be a direct sale? Will it be a subscription based method? With it be from advertising? For example, free mobile app games offer in-game purchases.

6. Key resources. This is all about what resources you will need for your business. What assets are key for your business? Think about finance, websites, team members or freelancers, email lists, manufacturing, marketing, branding, mentoring, coaching, intellectual property, suppliers, etc.

For example, McDonalds' key resources are team members and suppliers.

7. Activities. Think about the most important things you need to do in order to get your business model to work. What activities do you need to perform well? What do you need to become highly experienced in? Is it design? High quality services? Innovation? Marketing?

For example, I need to be able to teach to an incredibly high standard and create remarkable content for my company.

8. Partners. In this segment, think about who you can partner with, such as suppliers and joint venture partners. Partners can help you leverage your business model and turn it into something more powerful.

For example, I partnered with my investors to help my property business model grow. I am now partnering with highly experienced mentors for the Shifts to Success Business Accelerators for Police Officers.

9. Costs. Costs are a big part of your business model, so you need to think of all the costs associated with it. Think about fixed and variable costs and economy of scale.

For example, one cost for my company Shifts to Success is the hire of venues for our events.

Developing your unique Business Model Canvas as well as referring to your business plan will provide you with huge clarity and structure when you start your own business. However, we want to ensure you are protected when you do so.

Insurance

As I am sure you are fully aware as police officers, things can go wrong from time to time, despite our best intentions and efforts. It's essential that you have the right business insurance cover for your company, in particular public liability and professional indemnity insurance.

Most businesses need public liability insurance to protect them from potential compensation claims if they injure or damage another person or their property. Public liability insurance cover can be tailored to the risks particular to your company. This is important because it stops you from buying cover you don't need, or not enough cover.

Depending on your business, you might need to take out professional indemnity insurance. This type of cover is usually taken out if your business runs consulting services and offers advice to other people or companies. If the advice you have given is proven to have caused a financial loss or doesn't meet the expectations of your clients, you could be liable for a large compensation claim which could be financially crippling for your company.

Sadly, a compensation culture has become more popular in the world today. With this in mind, prepare your company in case it does face a claim.

Business insurance is something to think about right from the start of your business. You never know when a claim might be made against you, so ensure you get it sorted. There are many helpful brokerage websites online, or call a few advisors who can direct you to the right cover for your business.

ACTION. Another step I want you to take is to get a business interest form from your police force. Normally you can get one of these from your supervisor, the force intranet, or your professional standards department. To comply with police regulations you need to ensure that you fill one of these forms out and send it to the relevant department. If you do not, you may be summoned for a disciplinary hearing that may result in a dismissal.

My force's Professional Standards Department was very helpful when I sent my business interest form in. However, I do recommend you read the policy, which should be included as a document with the actual form, so as not to engage in anything the police service may deem unacceptable.

Do not put off filling in this form and sending it off to the relevant department. Once you have done it, it's out of the way.

Summary

We have covered a lot in this chapter. We now know what to include in our business plan; we understand different legal structures for our business and their benefits; we have learnt five different ways to come up with a company name; we know how to ensure we are maximising our available resources by cutting back on things; and we are setting up a business bank account. We have a template to map out our business model, providing us with clarity and structure, and we can correctly protect ourselves from any claims that may come our way.

In the next chapter we go on to the next step in building a successful business, Branding.

Success Story – Chris Latter

Chris Latter worked in the police force for thirteen years as a PC and a DC. After facing the many challenges the police go through (such as a demanding, stressful environment and family life being impacted) and becoming disillusioned with the job, he sought the advice of a close friend, Bob.

'Do what makes you happy,' he told Chris.

With the help of Bob, Chris came up with the type of business that would make him happy – landscaping. Sadly, Bob had been suffering from a brain tumour and has since passed away. As Chris was lowering his friend into his grave, he made a commitment right there and then: he was going to give his business a good go. He knew life was way too short to be anything but happy.

Chris started working on his business in his spare time. He built it up so he could leave the police force, and then joined Shifts to Success.

Since then, Chris has:

- Scaled his business to over £100,000 in sales per year
- Acquired a customer base that continues to grow
- Been invited to speak on *Gardeners' World* Live 2020
- Set up successful marketing campaigns
- Enjoyed a healthier and happier life beyond the police

I asked Chris how his life has changed.

Where to start? The business has grown a lot, achieving £100,000 turnover year-on-year. Shifts to Success has given me the confidence to tackle anything and push myself out of my comfort zone on Facebook Live, YouTube… the list is endless.

I would have never contemplated doing these things if I hadn't enrolled in Shifts to Success. It has made me look at different avenues I would never have looked at, or had the balls to look at, and I have learned more from the mentors and cohort members in the short space of time since I joined than I had at any point since starting the business. My sales, marketing, confidence – everything has improved.

I now do what I love and have no fear of what may or may not happen. I just want people to know that they shouldn't stick in a job they hate because of the security (like I did for thirteen years). My wife works part-time, we have two young children, I'm the main earner, but I still managed to make the jump and have continued to succeed. If I can do it with a VW Polo and a few gardening tools, anyone can.

People said I couldn't and shouldn't do it. I did it to prove to myself that I could. That's the drive I now have. You only live once. Do what makes you happy.

Chapter 6

Branding

'*Your brand is the heart of your business. You are the heart of your brand*'

Luke Vincent

Key learning points from this chapter:

- Generating ideas for your brand
- How to create an online presence
- How to be authentic to gain true followers
- Self-promotion
- Your story is value
- Your reason why is powerful

I firmly believe that your personal brand is also your company brand. They are both entwined. People like to connect with people, not just a logo.

For example, when you think of Steve Jobs, what brand do you think of? What about Elon Musk? Or Sir Richard Branson? Your personal brand will be combined with your company brand, which is a good thing because you get to express your own uniqueness through your company.

Everything you do impacts your brand in a positive or negative way, from the posts you like to the conversations you engage in. For example, people who do nothing but moan on Facebook subtract from their personal brand. Everything about you is a brand if you want to become a successful entrepreneur.

> '*Branding is about aligning everything you do with everything you say and your image. This is how you build a brand.*'
>
> Sapna Pieroux, brand consultant and design coach, founder of InnerVisions ID

A brand is something that your customers feel when they hear your or your company's name. To be successful in business, you need to make sure the thoughts and feelings they have are positive. A brand is your promise to your customers. It tells your target customers what they can expect from you, your products and services. So, it is a good idea to ensure these promises align well with your potential customers.

A brand is more than just a fancy logo. When you effectively implement a brand strategy, it can give you a huge edge in competitive markets.

> '*Your brand is what people think and feel about your business. What people think and feel affects what actions they take. This can be the difference between them choosing you or someone else. Between arguing over price or happily bringing you referrals. Think about*

that for a minute. It would be nice if it was something simple and tangible like a logo. But it's not; it is so much more than that. To manage your brand, you need to manage what people think and feel about you.'

Luke Vincent, brand and purpose strategist, founder of BeLucent

Recently I read an amazing book called *Shoe Dog* by Phil Knight, the founder of Nike. I recommend you read it too.

Nike has an emotional attachment to its customers when they wear Nike trainers. The company wants its footwear to make its customers feel like athletes, and it does a good job of transferring this emotion from its product to its customer.

Defining your brand as an entrepreneur is a fun and creative path of self-discovery. Next, I am going to share with you strategies to help you find your own amazing brand.

Generating ideas for your brand

Coming up with ideas for your brand is a process that requires some thought, but inspiration is all around you. It's your job to pick out what you want your brand to look, feel and sound like to help with the success of your business.

A great place to start is to ask yourself what adjectives would best describe your business. For example, I came up with supportive, transforming and driven for Shifts to Success. Once you have these words, search for things that align well with them to help you come up with ideas for the way you want your business and brand to look. One way to do this is to go online and pick out websites that you like. They don't have to be websites that are in the same industry as your business.

Another great way to come up with brand ideas is to create a mood board of anything that you like the look of, such as colours, logos and fonts. The ideas for your mood board can come from online or offline. Soon enough, you will see common themes. Pick out the most common two to three colours and from these create a colour palette. From this colour palette, which represents your brand and business, you can design your website, logo and social media account. It's important that your colours stay consistent throughout your business, otherwise it can confuse your market and customers.

You also want to refer back to your business plan to come up with brand ideas. Looking at your mission and values, the benefits and solutions your business has to offer, and your target market or niche will help you pick out what's important when it comes to your brand. Remember your market research, too, and it's a good idea to look at what you have named your company for inspiration for your brand.

There are different ways to design a logo. Don't worry – you don't have to be great at art. However, it is a good idea to sketch down a rough drawing of what you would like your logo to look like. You can hire a freelance graphic designer or branding expert to do this for you, but the latter can increase costs.

To help your logo stand out, use a simplistic design. For example, Apple has a very simple logo that the world recognises straight away, as do Nike and McDonalds. That said, make sure there is something unique about your logo design, too.

It's important to remain consistent with your logo throughout your business. You do not want different variations of it.

If you feel as though your company name and logo aren't telling your market enough about your business, you can add a tagline into the mix including the primary benefits of your company or your USP. Below are a few examples:

- Subway – Eat fresh
- Nike – Just do it
- McDonalds – I'm lovin' it
- L'Oréal – Because you're worth it
- Tesco – Every little helps
- Apple – Think different
- BMW – The ultimate driving machine
- HSBC – The world's local bank
- Gillette – The best a man can get

Ask your market if they like your brand, including the colours, logo and overall design. You will have a good indication from their response if you are on the right track or not. I wouldn't advise asking friends and family as they will typically want to compliment your new brand. You want honest and reliable feedback from the people you intend to serve, so send out a poll or survey to your email subscription list. This has the additional benefit of making them feel as though they are a part of your business and their opinion matters.

Once you have your values, mission, colour palette, logo, fonts and tagline, it's time to create an online presence with your brand.

How to create an online presence

Often people tell me they can't attract joint venture partners and raise finance. It's not hard to realise why. Their profile pictures on social media show them on a lads' holiday holding a beer can or at a festival covered in glow paint. They engage in online arguments that have nothing to do with their business or share posts about how bad their life is. This kind of behaviour doesn't help a brand; it damages it. Only post things that are relevant to your company and brand. If your company has nothing to do with politics, then don't post stuff about politics.

A great way to create a healthy online presence for your brand is to stay consistent. Don't have different names on different social media platforms, and remember to use the same type of theme from your branding ideas for your messaging. Remain professional on everything, from your social media to your website, and stick to a relevant email address that represents your company such as alex@shiftstosuccess.com.

Another great way to create a healthy online presence for your brand is to have an 'About' or 'Why' page on your website and social media platforms. Highlight what you stand for, what credibility you have and what experiences you can offer. Communicate what you and your company do in a clear and confident manner.

Customer reviews and testimonials have a positive impact. I appreciate you may not have these at the beginning, but a quick way to get them is to provide as much value as possible to a customer for free in exchange for a testimonial. As your business and brand grow, it's important to share any media or publications you may have been featured in, such as magazines, popular blog sites or interviews. When you are starting out, pitch your business to a media or publication company to help you get featured.

A powerful strategy is to pick one social media platform that is relevant to your company and dominate that platform. Provide as much high quality value as possible, such as blog posts, uploaded images and videos, to help gain a big following. It also helps to engage with your market on a regular basis and build a relationship with them. So many people just hit the 'like' button on Facebook, Instagram or YouTube. Call people by their name, ask them questions or add more value. Take the time to do this and it will pay you back tenfold.

'A big piece of the social puzzle is understanding where you need to have a voice. For example, are you a brand delivering a product or service that's highly visual? If so then jump on platforms like Instagram, Pinterest, Facebook and Twitter then weave them all together. Or maybe you're in an industry that's more White Collar and professional services related...In which case LinkedIn would be an important medium for you. Know what your brand is, where your ideal clients are and engage in a way that's socially applicable to your ideal audience.'

Josh Smith, co-Founder of We Fill Events

By creating an online presence, you will attract more customers than your competitors because you will be known within the market and deemed valuable due to the content you are providing. Once you are deemed valuable, you can increase your fees because you will be oversubscribed for products and services.

Think about Louis Vuitton making huge sales of bags that cost £3,000+ when there are bags in the market for £50 that look better and are just as practical. It is because customers believe Louis Vuitton bags are more valuable.

So how do you get your followers or market to believe in you in the first place? It all starts with being authentic.

How to be authentic to gain true followers

When you're building a brand, it is highly important that you act like the real you, otherwise people will feel as though something is off. Of course, it is important to remain professional, but that doesn't mean you have to become a fake. For example, entrepreneur Gary Vaynerchuk swears a lot in his content, including his keynote speeches. In spite of this, he is loved by millions of people around the world and has built up an incredible brand by being real.

People don't want another bland person in the marketplace; they want someone who is refreshingly real and transparent. Share your mistakes, tell relevant jokes (no matter how bad they are), share your opinions and embarrassing stories and do not hide who you are.

When I first watched an ad on YouTube for the Dollar Shave Club featuring the founder Michael Dubin, I was instantly drawn to the company. His ad has had over 24 million views on YouTube because it is a true representation of his brand. It made me feel connected with Michael even though I do not know him personally. The ad is direct, funny, honest, unpolished and authentic, and that is why it is so popular.

When you act with authenticity, you will repel the people who don't like you and your business, and attract the people who do. This is a win-win. You cannot get everyone to like you, so don't waste time trying. It's a path to mediocrity.

When you start building your business, don't worry about using content or topics that have already been published by other people. You can create authenticity for your brand by putting your uniqueness into it. Challenge yourself to express your authenticity in five different ways. For example, instead of using the word 'hello', greet people in different ways such as 'hey', yo', 'hi', 'good day' and 'hey-up'.

Tell your stories, and don't be afraid to share them through self-promotion.

Self-promotion

Some entrepreneurs feel that self-promotion sounds like they are bragging. I disagree. It is your duty as an entrepreneur to share your successes and your product or service. If someone in the world has a problem, no matter how big or small, share how your product or service can help.

When you have created something of value, be proud of it and express that through your brand. If you do something great, your customers want to know about it. Think of self-promotion as a service you can provide to your customers. If you don't self-promote, you are stealing something that could impact them in a positive way. Also, if you do not self-promote and your competitors do, then they have the advantage.

You can self-promote by sharing your successes through personal stories. For example, you could share a story of how you made your product and the reasons why you created it. When your customers used it, they got certain results which helped them become XYZ. Be mindful, however, that you don't share a success that happened twenty years ago. Make it recent.

When you do self-promote, ensure you back up your claims, because sooner or later your customers will find out if you are spouting false claims. This can be very damaging to your brand as customers will build a perception that you are unethical.

Your story is value

Sharing a personal story is an effective way of adding authenticity to your brand and building trust as you are letting people into your world. People don't only want to hear about your success. When I first shared my story in 2016 to 150 people at one of my business presentations, the compliments, emails and Facebook messages I received were truly inspiring.

At the age of ten, I saw my mum and dad arguing like I had never seen before. Then all of a sudden, my dad grabbed my mother. I don't think I had ever sworn up until that point, but I remember shouting, 'Fuck off, Dad,' then running upstairs and hiding under my bed.

He came upstairs and pulled me from under the bed.

Standing me to attention, he said, 'You don't swear at your dad.'

What happened next was one of the most heartbreaking things I have ever been through. My dad just got up and left our home, our lives. My brother was two years old at the time so he didn't really have an idea of what was happening, but I knew. Yet my hopes were high that my dad would return – this loving man who would wrestle with me after school, tickle me, tell me he loved me, was my protector.

It finally dawned on me that he wasn't coming back. My mum and dad had split up for good. I was broken. All I wanted was to see him and smell his aftershave and hear his laugh. But I couldn't.

At the age of seventeen, I was staying at a friend's house. During that night, my dad had come to visit my mum and she described the event as horrific. He had grabbed her and pushed her around the house until the police came and arrested him. When I heard of this, I felt an overwhelming respect for the police, and perhaps this was one of the reasons why I wanted to be a police officer. They saved my mum from a bad situation, and deep inside I thought maybe she would show me more love if I was a police officer.

Time went on, and as my relationship with my mother got worse, I fell into what I now know to have been depression. My mind wasn't in the right place and I wanted to kill myself. When I texted my mother to tell her this, the reply I got wasn't the most comforting – she didn't care.

My sadness turned to anger and I told myself enough was enough. Something had to change. I asked myself three questions: 'What have I achieved?', 'What have I become?'

and 'What have I created?' The answers were not inspiring, so I went on to Google and typed 'how to become rich'. Up came a book called *Think and Grow Rich*, by Napoleon Hill. About half way through this life-changing book I began to cry as I had finally found a way out of my current situation. Why had no one ever taught me this before? The way I thought determined my outcome.

Setting goals and working towards them was powerful in overcoming depression for me. The shifts I made in my mindset really helped me overcome the dark thoughts I had, and I can honestly say that since then, those thoughts have not come back. I believe they never will.

Having my story resonating with my company's reason why is a powerful driving force behind my brand. Ask yourself what stories you have, negative or positive, that can inspire people in your business industry. Remember your story has value.

Your reason why is powerful

There is a great book by Simon Sinek called *Start With Why* in which he explains that 'people do not buy what you do, they buy why you do it'. Having your own reason why at the forefront of your brand can be an extremely powerful technique to gain your target market's attention.

Of course, you can have more than one reason why you are doing what you are doing. Remember, being authentic is key. A huge reason why I started my company, Shifts to Success, was to extend an opportunity for police officers to find an alternative path in life. I believe that by supporting police officers to become successful entrepreneurs, I can impact our planet in a positive way.

If you start your own company, what will your reason why be? Know this why and incorporate it into your company to create a powerful brand that will attract more people to you and your mission.

Summary

Building a strong brand can have many positive effects on you and your company. Come up with ideas for your brand and create a strong online presence. Be refreshingly authentic.

Self-promotion is important to help build your brand. Share your personal story to add value and know why you are doing what you are doing in building your own company.

In the next chapter, we are going to cover the fourth element in my Business Builder Model, Implementation.

Success story – Victoria McDonald

Victoria McDonald had been in the police for over twelve years as a PC. She had no previous business experience, but knew she wanted to seek new opportunity – not so much to leave the police, but to give herself the option.

Victoria decided to attend a Success QuickStart Day to see if she could bring her business idea about interior design to life. She joined Shifts to Success and her results have been pretty amazing. She is now the founder of Quirk & Colour, an interior design company that has enabled her to:

- Make thousands of pounds in sales
- Come off antidepressant medication
- Run marketing assets and generate leads successfully through her content

I asked Victoria what kind of impact joining Shifts to Success has had on her life:

This whole process has given me more confidence in myself and really made me think about what I want from life, and given me the push I needed to ignore the naysayers and go after what I want.

My mindset has changed in all areas of my life. I began the process as a depressed police officer; I've now graduated as the owner and founder of an interior design business and been able to come off my depression medication just eight months in. This is monumental, and the knock-on effect has been immense. I will maintain and carry this through into wherever I go from here.

Before joining Shifts to Success, I knew what I wanted to do, but it seemed destined to be a pipe dream. It seemed too much of a mountain to scale, and I didn't know where to start. From the moment I joined the cohort, I made a promise to myself that I was going to follow the process, and that's how I have achieved what I have. I've learned to trust and go with my gut, ignore negativity and put myself first.

For the first time in several years, I'm really excited and looking forward to the future. My family and friends have all noticed my improved mindset and that I'm happier now I'm following my dream. What I've learned has improved my time planning and organisation tenfold. My procrastination has decreased dramatically, and I enjoy the benefits of being a healthier, happier me.

Chapter 7

Implementation

'*The leverage and influence social media gives citizens are rapidly spreading into the business world.*'

Simon Mainwaring

Key learning points:

- Tale of the two brothers
- Leveraging systems
- Creating content – building trust
- Capturing leads
- Building relationships
- Social media marketing

A tale of two brothers

There were once two brothers, Bion and Cylon, who lived in ancient Greece in 100BC. Their father, the great King Aktor, ruled the lands where they lived.

One day King Aktor summoned his two sons to his royal halls, along with the people of the land. There was going to be an announcement that everyone must hear from the king himself.

The king set out a challenging but rewarding task for his sons to build two huge statues in honour of their father. Whichever son completed the task first would be rewarded with kingship, all the riches the land had to offer and a life of luxury. However, each son must complete the task alone and compete against each other to see who was truly worthy of the kingship.

The two brothers, both twenty-one years of age, knew the task would take years to complete. But nonetheless, each brother was excited as the reward was truly great and they would get to honour their father in front of his people.

Bion began to work on the task immediately. He slowly dragged huge, heavy and difficult to manoeuvre boulders into position, as per the drawings his father had given him. After a few months, the base of his statue was nearly in place. The people of the land gathered to applaud Bion for his amazing efforts.

However, Bion was bewildered as the plot of land his brother Cylon had been given to build his own statue on lay empty. Not a single boulder had been moved into position; in fact, there was still vegetation growing on the land. Intrigued and confused, Bion went to visit Cylon's home, finding him in his hut working on a horrible looking contraption that resembled something from the execution chambers in the town.

Bion was annoyed and shouted, 'Cylon, are you crazy? We have a task to do for Father, and yet you lie here, playing around making horrible looking contraptions. This isn't a game!'

Cylon smiled at his brother. 'Leave me alone, Bion, I am building my own statue.'

Bion laughed. 'Yeah, right, it looks like that, you fool. You haven't laid a boulder. Father will be angry when he finds out you are not taking his task seriously.'

Another six months passed and Bion continued to work on his statue. Now the second level was nearly in place, but here Bion encountered a problem. He was starting to struggle with the work, finding it extremely difficult to haul the huge boulders into the last few positions of the second phase. Troubled by his limitations, Bion held a competition to find out who amongst the people of the land could lift the heaviest of the boulders. In return, he would give that man many riches when he became king.

Dexios won the competition as the town's strongest man. Dexios then helped Bion with the large, heavy boulders and lifted them to higher levels of the statue.

Bion looked over from the second level of the statue to see if his brother Cylon had become wise to the idea of building his own statue. To his shock, he found that not a single boulder had been positioned into place. Bion was saddened by the sight as he thought his brother respected their father more than that.

Eventually, Bion forgot about his brother as he continued his hard labour on his own statue. Another year passed, but half way through the third phase of Bion's creation, his work came to a demoralising crawl. It was now taking Bion three months to move a single boulder, despite all the help he was getting from the town's strongest man, Dexios. In addition to this, Bion was spending his monetary resources on nutritional plans to help build his strength for the tiresome work.

Over lunch, Bion and Dexios discussed their plans for the statue and worked out it would take another ten years before the monument was complete for the king. Bion exclaimed, 'We will get there one day! We just need to keep working. My brother, Cylon, has yet to lay a single boulder. What a fool!"

Suddenly Bion heard a loud commotion coming from the town centre. The people of the land, who normally watched Bion's amazing efforts, quickly left as their curiosity got the better of them. Bion was also curious and abandoned his work with Dexios to check out what was making so much noise.

Fighting through the crowd, Bion got to see what all the fuss was about. His brother Cylon was pushing a large contraption, that contained within it wheels, levers and ropes, through the town centre, towards the empty plot of land his father had given him. Bion feared the worst, and his fears were confirmed when his brother came to a halt. Within minutes, Cylon's weird machine was laying the base of the statue, boulder by boulder. It lifted with ease the boulders that had taken Bion weeks or months to move, and before long it had the entire foundation laid. All Cylon had to do was pull a rope which turned the machine's cogs and wheels, and hey presto! The boulders were moved with pace and precision.

After two weeks, Cylon moved on to the second phase of the statue, and within a week he had completed it. Bion was devastated, but instead of looking to build his own machine or leveraging some other means to beat his brother, he decided he must get stronger and get other strong men from the town to help him.

After just over two years, Cylon completed his monument – two years to build his machine and a few weeks to reap the benefits. The great King Aktor was extremely happy with his son, and as promised rewarded Cylon with kingship and riches. Cylon never worked another day in his life.

The fantasy story above demonstrates that the old way of thinking – going through tiresome labour for many years – is not a good strategy at all. Using systems to leverage your time and work will far exceed you doing the all the work yourself.

Systems are a crucial part of business success and are what this chapter is all about. We live in extraordinary times where tasks that would have taken days, weeks and months to complete now can take us minutes. If you want to become a successful entrepreneur away from the police service, you will need to develop systems into your business.

But what is actually possible by leveraging systems?

Leveraging systems

Systems are simple to use, can be repeated and are predictable. In July 2017, I launched a product leveraging certain systems that has had an incredible return on investment (ROI). I decided to create an information product for investors to help them succeed in the property industry. I then engaged with my niche market on a regular basis, providing them with valuable free information that would help them move that bit closer to their desired outcome, but for them to receive this free information, they would have to opt in and provide me with their email addresses. The systems I used automated this process to ensure I wasn't trading my time collecting these email addresses. Eventually I had over 1,000 people on my email list. I also used platforms like Facebook to let people know that I was creating something valuable and free, which caused a buzz within my niche market.

I gained some phenomenal results. From the people on my email list, 4% bought my product, so I made forty sales. My product cost £297, which generated an income from this product launch of £11,880.

The most fascinating thing about this result is that the product only took me seventeen hours to create. It was inexpensive to formalise into a PDF document, using someone else's expertise, and the systems I used were automatic. I generated this income from the comfort of my own home.

How many hours as a police officer would it take to earn £11,880?

This is what is possible when you use the correct systems to leverage your time. Let's look at a couple more examples.

Let's say you have your own email list of 1,000 people. According to The Radicati Group's Email Statistics Report, 2012–2016, there are around 4.3 billion email addresses, so gaining 1,000 email addresses for your list is more than achievable. Now let's say you sell a premium product for £2,000, but you only covert 2% of your list into sales. That's twenty sales, and twenty sales at £2,000 per sale = £40,000.

Let's say you then create a subscription-based product. This is a product your customers pay you each month for, examples being Netflix, The Dollar Shave Club or Graze. Eighty-five people decide to pay you for your product at £50/month = £4,250 per month. That is £51,000 per year.

How many years would it take you to reach that income in the police service? How many hours? What rank would you need to achieve? I can assure you, the answers won't even come close to the earning potential of leveraging systems.

Entrepreneur and co-Founder of We Fill Events, Josh Smith, explained that by consulting the directors of a major sporting team in Australia, he helped them realise they had an untapped database consisting of tens of thousands of emails and phone numbers. In one quick marketing ploy, they were able to whip up a campaign that created a huge spike in ticket sales for their next home match, surpassing all their records and turning sales worth $800ish into $20,000+ inside twenty-four hours.

Your database of email addresses is a critical component of your asset base for your business. It will help you to create cash windfalls as you need them in between your business's core sales, and will open up the opportunity to add value to your community. This in turn will lift you to being the go-to leader that clients will trust and stick with for years to come.

Please be aware that making an income online from your

business is only one way of doing so. There are a number of different ways to generate sales which we will go into in Chapter 9, but for now it's all about content creation.

Creating content – building trust

There are four different forms of content:

- Video – YouTube, Instagram, Facebook or Periscope
- Audio – people can listen to audio content such as podcasts on iTunes and Sound Cloud when they're on the go
- Written – on blog posts, websites and social media
- Images – on platforms such Instagram and Pinterest

The whole aim is to get your target market to know, like and trust you so they will provide you with their email address and ultimately buy from you. The way entrepreneurs do this is to create high quality content that helps their target market while ensuring they are truly authentic. We will go deeper into this in the Prospecting section of Chapter 9.

> '*Gone are the days of communicating business to business (B2B), gone are the days of communicating business to consumer (B2C). We now live in an era where we have to communicate H2H, heart to heart, in order to get our market to know, like and trust us.*'
>
> Tim Han, international speaker, entrepreneur, online marketing wizard and founder of Success Insider

A great way to create content is to understand what your target clients' problems are. What difficulties do they have?

What challenges are they facing? What do they want to gain for themselves? Once you know these things, you can then create content based upon them.

There is structure I use to help me create content in a strategic way:

The first step is simple. Explain who you are, what you do and how you help people.

Next, you need to resonate with them. Ask questions such as, 'Do you have this problem? or 'Have you ever wondered why you have this problem?' or 'Are you facing these challenges?' These questions are 'hooks' that capture the attention of your target market. Remember you want to communicate heart to heart with your market, and by starting off with their issues, problems and challenges, you will be doing that.

Share with your target market frustrations, challenges, difficulties and problems you have faced. Remember, every pro was once an amateur. It's good to share a story here if possible, and it doesn't have to be about you. You can share other people's stories, letting your target clients know why you have an interest in giving them the content you're about to give them. You will then have common ground with them.

Next, share how you found a solution or positive outcome to a challenge or problem you faced. Talk about the things you did leading up to finding the solution.

After that, share how your life changed as a result of finding the solution, or how other people's lives changed.

Share the step-by-step guide or structure that brought you to the solution. This is where you give the most valuable part of the content away, teaching your target market the specifics to help them with their issues, problems, challenges and frustrations.

Finally, direct your audience with a call to action. If the goal is to gain email addresses, you want them to opt in and provide their details in return for something of value. It's a good idea here to ask your target market to subscribe to your social media channels.

Don't worry about trying to be perfect when you are creating content. The most important thing is to get started. Once you have target clients' email addresses, you can then engage with them and build relationships.

Also, don't worry about not having the right camera equipment if you are choosing the video form of content. Start with whatever resources you have. The more you do of it, the better you will become. Content creation is a skill you need to develop as an entrepreneur, so enjoy the process and let your creative juices flow.

I would recommend you create a content calendar. You generally want to release content to your email list at least once a week, so it's important that you get a schedule going and ensure you keep to it. A tip I found useful was to film or write several pieces of content so I was ahead of myself.

When you know how to conduct market research, you can easily plan your content creation. Next to the numbers one to fifty-two to represent the weeks of the year, write the topic you will be releasing each week to your email list. The topics you plan now can change, so at this stage just get something down that is relevant to your target market. Relevant is the key word here – there is no point talking about football if your business is in the musical arts industry.

Here is an example for a business in the health industry:

1. Learn the top five nutritional benefits of a low-carb diet
2. How to build muscle with three easy steps.
3. How to burn more fat with these five secrets
4. The top ten habits for a healthier lifestyle
5. Seven tips for gaining more energy in your life

I have included numbers in each of the topics above. Numbers aren't necessary, but they are a great hook to increase the chances of your market reading or watching the content.

There are other types of content you can create too, such as:

- Step by step and how-tos
- Case studies of people who have gained results from your product or service
- Inspirational thought pieces to improve mindset
- Interviews
- 'Ask the audience' pieces, where you ask your audience what topics they want you to cover

The purpose of the content calendar is to provide you with structure and a planning format, so that you know exactly what content you need to produce and when. This way there is no excuse for not getting your content delivered.

An added benefit of creating content is that you only have to create it once and you can use it on various platforms. For example, you can film your content for YouTube or Facebook, then get the film transcribed into a written format for a blog post on your website. Designers can pick out quotes from your written content to create pictures for platforms such as

Instagram, and freelancers to pull audio from the film and convert it into MP3 for a podcast. Repurposing your content and using it in multiple different ways is a productive way to get yourself and your company known in your business industry. This will increase the chances of your content being shared, as long as the content you are creating is of high quality.

Remember, content is king. The more relevant, high quality content you create for your target market, the more you can drive that market to your opt-in page.

Next, we will learn how to capture leads to build your email list.

Capturing leads

A highly important part of content that entrepreneurs often forget to add is a call to action. By including a strong call to action in every piece of content, you dramatically increase the chances of your market providing their email addresses on your opt-in page.

Social media and blog/vlog platforms are game changers for businesses. You can run ads for a competitive price compared to radio, newspaper and TV. An added benefit is that you can target your ads specifically to ensure the market you want to engage with actually sees the content you are providing them with.

A simple structure on how an email marketing system works is as follows:

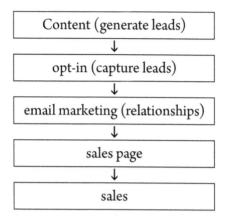

There are numerous names for an opt-in page, such as squeeze page or landing page, but the objective is the same: to capture email addresses from your target market. The idea behind this is that you can then send more high quality content, ideas, updates and promotions to your target clients.

I asked international speaker, world-renowned coach and online marketing expert Tim Han why he thinks building an email list is important for your business. He explains:

> *I believe it comes down to retention. When you're building an email list, you generally do so because you're building up value and you're adding value into other people's lives. And when you do this, prospects that join your email list are more likely to stick around to do business with you. This is something I like to call 'Getting clients and cash-flow for life'.*
>
> *You do this by nurturing them by delivering consistent and constant value through the email inbox. For example, when you subscribe to one of my businesses called Success Insider, I'm constantly sending blog posts and free value because the*

more they keep seeing my name, the more they just want to do business with me when a certain problem or pain point strikes for them. That inevitably means conversion, meaning I make money.

So, increasing conversion means increasing sales for your business, and also it is important to build an email list because it is traffic that you own. For example, it's great when you're on Facebook and you are advertising on there and building up a following, but what happens when Facebook decides to change something that results in them wiping you off their platform? Well, then you have lost all that traffic unfortunately because Facebook owns that traffic. So, email is powerful because you're building your own traffic and that's the thing you own, and you can drive your traffic anywhere and everywhere that you want to. So ultimately traffic that you own in terms of email addresses you have collected on to your subscription list is one of the main points of why it's so important to build an email list in the first place. Ownership.

Some sort of free gift has to be on offer in exchange for an email address, and the gift has to be attractive to your target market. Normally this is an information-based gift as information is inexpensive to create. Gifts can be in the form of a quiz relevant to your target market, an eBook, video series or download. If you want to check out an example, you can head to shiftstosuccess.com where you can find the free gift I offer as well as an opt-in on my homepage.

Once you have gained an email address from your target market, you need to start building a relationship with them.

Building relationships

Before people buy from you, they need to know, like and trust you. When people provide you with their email address, they take a step closer to knowing what you and your business have to offer. You do not want to rush in and push a product or service in their face, as this may prompt them to unsubscribe from your email list. You want to provide more value and build towards a stronger relationship.

For this you can use an emailing platform such as MailChimp, AWeber or GetResponse which will host the addresses you have been collecting. Pick a platform that suits your needs as they have different benefits and pricing.

Emailing platforms will allow you to communicate with your email list on a regular basis. Consistency is important here. You do not want to send out three emails in one week, then another one a month later. To make consistency easy, automate the process of sending out your emails via the emailing platform you decide to work with. Your content calendar should come in handy here too.

You may hear the term 'funnel', which is basically the process you take your potential customers through, like a journey. As they go on this journey you will provide them with value and you will nurture them, so that ultimately they will buy from you. There are various other funnels to help you with your email marketing process and ultimately make sales, but the main point is that you have to ensure that you are sending free, relevant, high-quality content to your audience regularly in order to cultivate a relationship with them. The key to this is to have an online presence aside from your own website. Use social media marketing to your advantage.

Social media marketing

I like to think of social media as a microphone. Imagine Taylor Swift singing in a huge concert hall like the O2 Arena without a microphone. How many people do you think would hear her voice clearly? Not many. Compare that to her having the correct audio equipment as well as her microphone. Yep, now everyone can hear her.

That is what social media can do for you in business: it can amplify your mission, services, products, message and content around the world.

There are various different platforms you can use to help you generate leads, such as Facebook Ads, Google Retargeted Ads, YouTube, Instagram, and Twitter. Tim Han has had huge success on YouTube. Within a couple of days of him posting a video, 2,000 webinar registrants had opted in. That's why social media can be so powerful.

As times change and technology blossoms, the attention of the population is no longer on TV, radios, newspapers or magazines. The majority of people's attention is on smartphones. A study led by Nottingham Trent University asked participants aged eighteen to thirty-three to estimate the amount of time they spend on their phone and compare their estimates to their actual usage. The study discovered that the average person checks their device eighty-five times a day, spending a total of five hours browsing the web and using apps. This equates to around a third of the time a person is awake. Knowing this, we can prepare to grab the attention of our target market with our high quality content.

There are other methods of marketing for your business, such as:

- Events
- Adverts (offline)
- Affiliates
- Ambassadors
- SEO (search engine optimisation)

To get started, though, you may want to use social media marketing as a core strategy. It allows you to build a loyal community of followers, as people like to be a part of a business with a lively community. This will help you establish an emotional connection with your market which will support your long-term success.

Social media is also an amazing feedback source. It enables your market to communicate with each other as well as your business, which improves your customer service as a company. Great customer service is a powerful marketing tool to generate leads. Interacting on different social media platforms, you will support your digital exposure for your company. Social media is worldwide and has immense sharing capabilities.

Compared to traditional channels of marketing like print advertising, social media marketing won't break the bank. The actual platform itself is free, and when you do run ads, you have complete control over your budget on a daily basis. If you don't want to put too much time into social media marketing, you can always outsource. There are some great companies that focus solely on social media marketing.

Summary

Don't be like Bion and work your life away, not being truly rewarded for your efforts. It's not always about who works the hardest, it's about leveraging systems. Content is important for your business and will help you generate and capture leads. You can amplify your content reach through social media.

It's now time to add extra value into your customers' lives by creating products and services for them.

Success story – Jamie Stenton

Jamie Stenton has worked for the police for over twenty years, first as a PC, then as a DI. Wanting more control of his life and to help his mother in business, Jamie decided to join Shifts to Success with no previous business experience. He now helps run his family business Lilac James, a digital marketing agency.

Within twelve months, Jamie:

- Systemised the business
- Gained high-profile clients
- Increased profits by 215%
- Increased product prices by 200%
- Gained over £100,000 in sales
- Enjoyed the biggest revenue and profit period in the business's ten-year history

Jamie explains:

Overall, since joining Shifts to Success, I have managed to change the business significantly, successfully attracting a higher level of client, raising prices and improving the services we offer. The business has moved from being in a precarious position (struggling to pay VAT, corporation tax and building refurbishment costs) to being consistently and healthily in profit each month. The future looks bright, the main challenge now being to manage the growth, rather than just getting by.

I asked Jamie what has changed for him personally since joining Shifts to Success and growing the business.

I'm now a real asset to the business. I feel capable and competent to advise on a range of strategic business issues, not just for my own business, but for many others too. I'm immensely proud of how far my knowledge and ability have come in twelve months, and I no longer feel like a one-trick pony with skills that can only be used within the policing profession. What I learned and experienced within the police is valuable to the private sector too.

I'm also understanding who I am. For a long time, my identity was attached to my role as a police officer. I was constrained by the limits that role places on personalities and opinions. Since joining Shifts to Success and expanding my life outside of the police, I've re-identified with myself to a far greater degree and am quickly learning who I am, what I want and what I'm capable of.

I feel content that my mum will have a sustainable retirement, and I will have options and skills outside of the police service. The biggest impact upon my family is that I can pass these skills on to my children and encourage an entrepreneurial attitude and development in them. I can guide them through business start-up and assist them with their mindset.

Chapter 8

Products

'Great companies are built upon great products'

Elon Musk

Key learning points from this chapter:

- Information products
- Key benefits of information products
- Achieving six figures through your products
- Integrated product suites

Information products

One of the most valued commodities in this day and age is knowledge. Billions of people around the world are consuming information on a daily basis. Your smartphone can now tell you the latest football scores or what the weather is going to be like this week, or even show you live video.

More and more people are deciding not to attend university. I for one prefer information programmes that provide me with specialised knowledge, or I simply google what I want to learn. Think about the last time you used Google or another online platform to learn how to do something. Back before we had the internet, this information would have been passed from person to person. It may have taken days to get the information to the person who wanted to learn it. Now if people want to learn something to improve their life or solve a problem, the relevant information is always within reach. Take advantage of this as a business owner and create information products for your customers.

Of course there are physical products that you could create, but the cost and risk can be much higher than when you create an information product (however, do not discard the concept of physical products if you have a specific idea for one) With a physical product, you have to ensure that your product will actually sell, because if it doesn't, you are burdened with stock that no one wants, and that stock has to be stored. You also have to think about your manufacturers and the cost implications of creating the product in the first place.

Information products and digital courses teach your customers something that they didn't know before or relieve some sort of pain they are going through. There are other benefits to your product that will be a part of your USP. If you think that you don't know anything of value, I believe that you do. You just need to know how to package it as a product. But as with anything, if you want to earn more, I would suggest you learn more about a particular skill.

Once you learn how to package a product, you have a

business asset you can direct your customers to. It can then produce a high amount of income for you and your business, and as an entrepreneur you will be providing value and helping people.

Key benefits of information products

Low risk. You are essentially creating highly valuable content that doesn't require a load of start-up capital. You won't need to go looking for investors to build your business. You can get started where you are financially, the only requirement being the time you'll need to create the product. As a police officer, your rest days will come in handy.

Saves time. With other business models, it may require a lot of time to implement your plans. However, with information products, you are generally working with what you already know, so you can take action much more quickly.

Passive income. I do not buy into the belief that business is 100% passive. If you are looking for that kind of business, then I am sorry to disappoint, because that is not what I am teaching. Entrepreneurship requires hard work.

However, I am a firm believer in working *on* your business and not *in* it. With information products that deliver value, you can automate systems so that your product can sell every hour of the day, 24/7, without you being there to sell it.

Phenomenal returns. Because you are not selling physical stock, you do not need to worry about huge overheads. So most of the income you generate will be pure profit, meaning that your ROI will be amazing.

Your ROI is your gross income divided by the total investment multiplied by 100. So if you were to spend £100 creating your information product and you priced that product at £300, for example, even if you only sold one product in a year, your ROI would be 300%, which is a phenomenal return.

Domination. With information products you can completely dominate a certain niche with a small list of customers, while other business models may need a large number of customers. This is because you can target your marketing to customers who really care about your work.

There are quite a few benefits to information products, but why would people buy from you? Your niche customers will develop a community that enables people to better themselves, ultimately bringing togetherness, interaction and engagement. I firmly believe that if you build relationships and cultivate an engaging community where you help and support people, they will buy from you.

Achieving six figures through your products

There are many inexpensive ways of developing your information product:

- PDFS
- EBooks
- Teleseminars
- Audio programmes
- Webinars/webcasts

- Subscription/membership sites
- Speeches
- Seminars
- Online/DVD courses
- Online consulting
- Online coaching
- Mastermind groups
- Mobile apps/tools

By focusing on three of these products, I am going to share with you how you can earn six figures from your business. These products are all low risk and will allow you to build momentum.

Monthly membership programme. Total product price – £348. Let's say that over a year, you get sixty people to enrol in your monthly membership programme, which costs £29 per month – £29 × 60 = £1,740 × 12 = £20,880 per year income. That would mean you would only need five people to sign up each month for your programme. Of course, the more people you get to sign up, the more your income increases.

A twelve-part webinar series. Total product price £1050: 24 people pay £87.50 per month for your twelve-part webinar series = £2,100 per month. Yearly income from this product is £2,100 × 12 = £25,200.

Online course. Total product price £3,564. Twenty people pay £297 a month for your online course = £5,940 per month. Yearly income from this product is £5,940 × 12 = £71,280.

All three products produce a yearly income of £117,360, and the best thing about it is you do not always have to find new customers for each product. Typically, people who buy one of your products will buy another if they are good value.

However, if you really want to scale your business, create an integrated product suite.

Integrated product suites

An integrated product suite is a buying journey that you take your customers on. More and more companies are going from a linear buying experience to a cyclical buying experience. Customers are buying into entire ecosystems that generally start off with a low barrier of entry, and that's how you build brand loyalty.

Think about each device and service that Apple offers. They are connected with all the other devices and services in multiple ways. Apple's products are functionally integrated and customers are so well served that the majority never leave the brand.

Gifts. This stage is to grab the attention of your customers in the form of completely free content such as blog posts, YouTube videos, podcasts or MP3 downloads. Having these gifts out in the marketplace will grab the attention of your niche and help drive them to your opt-in page to join your subscription list. Then you can begin to cultivate a relationship.

Low-tier. This stage offers a product that is a low barrier to entry, typically allowing your prospects to get to know you more by actually becoming customers. At this stage you want your customers to take that first step in buying into your product ecosystem.

Mid-tier. The idea behind this stage is to offer your customers your premium core offering. This is your main income generator for your business. The type of customers who will buy this product will know, like and trust you, and typically will have already bought from you in the low-tier stage. Your core offering must be remarkable and solve your customers' problem, whatever that may be. The pricing should reflect that.

High-tier. At this stage you will generally create a product that will continue the buying experience for your customer. Customers who buy this type of product are loyal and love previous products that they have bought from you. This is typically the highest priced product you will have.

Let's go back to Apple and look at its product ecosystem:

- Apple's gift is iTunes
- Apple's low-tier products are iPod and Apple watch
- Apple's mid-tier products are iPad and iPhone
- Apple's high-tier products are MacBooks, iMacs and towers

It's important to focus on core products with your business and not create hundreds of different products. You can add more later, when you have a profitable, sustainable business, but when you are starting out, I believe focusing on four types of product is critical. Integrate them with one another.

You don't need to overwhelm yourself and get all these products in place at the same time. Build one, sell it to your market, and then build the next tier of product.

When Steve Jobs came back to Apple in 1997 after the company's sales had dropped by 30%, the first thing he did was look at the product line. He soon realised that the focus was across several different products, so he reduced the product line by 70% and moved the billion dollar company's attention to four products' quality and innovation. Apple then went from a loss of $1.04 billion to turning a profit of $309 million.

Summary

Developing high quality products for your customers is essential for business success, and creating information-based products is a great place to start. Generating an annual six-figure income for your business may sound like it's pretty far away, but in actual fact it isn't, especially if you develop an integrated product suite to produce maximum profit.

Speaking of profits, let's get into Sales.

Success Story – Kelly Statham

Kelly Statham was a police officer for over ten years until she decided to leave the force for the sake of her mental health. She also wanted to become a better mother to her children.

Kelly went into business without the support of Shifts to Success and was making a £600 loss every month within the property industry as an estate and letting agent. She realised that she needed support and the correct insights on how to start and scale a business, so she made the decision to join Shifts to Success. Within one year, her business achieved £136,000 in revenue, and eighteen months on became a £250,000 business.

Kelly has won awards, been published in national magazines and, more importantly, is a better mother and wife. She now spends far more quality time with her family.

I asked Kelly what the impact has been on her life:

I now have a great income, I am much happier and more career-driven. I love getting up and going to work on my business. I'm also more confident in approaching customers.

I feel the strongest impact is the confidence and guidance Shifts to Success has given me. I have always been told that I can't do things, but this process has shown me that I can do things, and I will. I have learned to believe in myself and love myself. Not only that, but I spend more time with my family and feel better for it. My life has changed for the better and I am so excited for my and my family's future.

Chapter 9

Sales

'A plant doesn't grow without water and your prospects won't become customers without nurturing.'

James White

Key learning points:

- Understanding prospecting for your business
- Listen to your customers
- Closing the sale
- Using sale tactics

You will have to sell your product and service to your market. Without sales, a business doesn't exist.

Sales people typically have a bad name, mainly because of annoying, unwanted cold calls. However, as an entrepreneur, you will be selling your product or service to make your customers' lives better and ultimately solve a problem they have.

When I was seventeen, I worked in sales for three years.

The environment I was in involved both inbound and outbound calls, and I did pretty well if I do say so myself. At first, I hated the job, but once I started to see results, I thrived on it and learnt a lot about handling calls and objections that came my way.

For my property business, I sold property tour days to investors to show them around my portfolio and teach them about certain investing strategies. After a year of doing this I was able to generate an income of about £16,000pa. I sold these days either via face to face meetings or over the phone, learning a lot about the questioning phase of sales in the process.

You have to learn how to sell if you want to become a successful entrepreneur, no ifs, no buts. Thankfully, it is not a complex process, if you have followed the previous steps in my Business Builder Model. When you understand your market, you can easily make sales.

There are multiple ways to generate sales online and in person. Regardless of which one you choose, you will still need to cultivate a relationship with your market.

Understanding prospecting for your business

Prospecting is a term used in sales. It means finding the right customers for your products and services. This will then enable you to move them through the sales cycle, from cold to warm, to hot.

Cold prospects are people or companies you have identified as prospects, but they have little to no awareness of your company, product or services. Cold prospects are typically reached through marketing advertisements, networking and cold calling. With any type of prospecting, marketing will play a huge part.

I recommend you concentrate your marketing efforts on selective groups where you have the best chances of coming into contact with your niche market. Once you have cold leads on your database, you can then cultivate the relationships by maintaining consistent communication. Your prospects will then become warm.

Warm prospects are people you have previously spoken to or met who know about your company and the product and services you offer. Hot prospects are people who have successfully moved through the first two stages of the sales cycle via your marketing strategy. At the hot stage your prospects are more likely to buy so you can close the sale.

Grant Cardone, a master in sales, is an entrepreneur I truly admire. He always talks about keeping his pipeline (database) full of prospects, which enables him to make more sales. The more people you have on your database, the more sales you will make. Fill your pipeline by reaching out to as many cold prospects in your market as possible.

You can do this in many ways, but the way that yields the best results is creating content online. Grant states that obscurity is a mistake that people often make. You need to get yourself known in your business industry.

Creating content on a regular basis online gains you influence in your business industry and you will be looked upon as an expert. Create videos, blog posts, including guest posts, interviews, webinars, Facebook lives and emails. It is wise to place your content where you know your prospect will come across it.

There are three types of content I use to gain influence. The first is inspirational content, which helps my prospects feel something and take action to engage with me. The second is educational content, which works well because I am teaching people something they need to know. It also helps with search engine optimisation as generally people who want to find information type words such as 'How to build a business' into a search engine. The third type of content is community content, which showcases my community. This strategy is great because my community helps me come up with content ideas. Remember the objective of your content is to prospect potential customers on to your database.

You will also have to speak to your prospects directly, over the phone or in person. Even though the internet is a powerful tool, people do business with people. Once you have prospects on your database, arrange an appointment to meet with them in person, in a group meeting or via a Skype call. It doesn't matter which as long as you can see the prospect eye to eye. It is important to note that when you meet, you will create a sales environment. This will help your prospect know that now is their moment to buy. Do not try to sell your product over the phone, unless you have met the prospect previously and they are asking to buy from you right there and then.

When you're setting up an appointment, ensure that you are speaking to the decision maker. You do not want to commit to a meeting and conduct your amazing sales presentation only for your prospect to say, 'I've got to ask my boss,' or 'I've got to ask the wife'. A strategy you could use to set up a meeting is to assume the prospect will meet with you. Here's where you close them on the appointment. You could offer a choice of times, for example, 'Would you prefer to meet on Tuesday at ten or Wednesday at two?' or one specific time, 'I can meet with you Monday at 13.30. Is that okay with you?' Experiment and see which works for you. If the prospect says no, you can then name another date and time rather than assuming he or she turning you down entirely.

From time to time you will get objections from your prospects. This is normal, so do not worry. A way to overcome these objections is as follows:

YOU: Hi, (prospect's name), it is (your name) from (your company). Are you well?

PROSPECT: I am good, thanks.

YOU: We have spoken before by email and I notice you are on my email list and subscribe to my social media channels. I'd like to meet you in person. Do you have fifteen minutes spare so I can come and see you? Or if you prefer Skype, we can do that.

PROSPECT: I don't think it's necessary at the moment. I don't have the need for (your product or service).

YOU: I was hoping you would say that as it's actually best we meet before you have the need. It will save you time in the long run. This way I will be ready and prepared for you.

A huge common objection is, 'I am too busy.'
To counter this objection you could say, 'It will only take

ten minutes of your time,' or 'Why don't we book a brief meeting for a couple of months' time? I have my diary open now. When is a less busy time for you?'

Generally your prospect will arrange a meeting for the future.

Some prospects will refuse to meet with you. Don't take this to heart; move the prospect's information to another list and try them again in a couple of weeks, using a different approach. Most sales experts say keep trying until the prospect has said no three times. However, as you are building up a community and producing content on a regular basis, you will likely already have some level of rapport with your prospect.

Now it's time to understand a core principle in selling: shut up and listen!

Listen to your customers

During your sales meetings, it is vital that you listen carefully to what your prospects are saying. Too many business owners rush in and talk about their product or service, making the focus of the meeting all about them and their business. This is the wrong thing to do. The meeting should always be about your prospect. There is a rule I like to stand by which is that 30% of the time you speak and the other 70% allow your prospect to speak.

Ask questions of your prospects to find out more about their thoughts on buying your product or service. You will then get your prospect to do most of the talking, shift the focus from you to your prospect, delight your prospect because you are showing an interest, and help the prospect answer their own objections. This will enable you to gather further information which will lead to more questions. Your questions will probe and help you uncover real issues, and keep you from being on the back foot during the meeting. Your prospects will get emotionally involved as they talk about their pain points, and people generally buy with their emotions. The less you talk, the more you will sell.

It's important to avoid negative small talk at the beginning of the conversation. Do not mention how bad the weather is, how depressing the news or how tired you are. You need to set the tone and start off with something positive. Then move on to the first question, 'Do you mind if I ask you a few questions?'

Typically, your prospect will then say, 'Go ahead,' or 'That's fine'.

Follow up with questions that are relevant to your product or service, but ensure the questions are all about the prospect. Great questions to ask on the initial meeting are:

- Why are (your products/services) so important to you?
- If I had a magic wand, what would the ideal solution to your problem be?
- Would you mind sharing your problem with me so I can better understand it?
- Where do you want to be in twelve months' time?
- Where are you now? (What's going well, what's not going well?)
- What's holding you back from getting where you want to be?

- Is there anything I can add or change to meet your needs?

Your questions will be ideally suited to your prospect. By the end of the questions, it should be clear to the prospect that they could benefit from your product or service. Typically they will be on your database, so they will be pre-qualified prospects as they have shown some interest in your content. However, if you would like to qualify them further than through chatting to them over the phone, meeting with your prospect is no bad thing.

It is a good idea to write down the answers that your prospect gives you, but always ensure you make eye contact, nodding and letting them know that you are listening. Their answers are more data that will better prepare you for future meetings, your sales emails, your content, your product launches, and closing the sale in that particular meeting. A sales meeting is also an opportunity for your prospect to learn about you, so keep that in mind, too.

Block booking meetings is a great way to produce sales. You can set up a meeting with ten warm to hot prospects which will help you generate more sales in less time, or you can hold sales meetings individually one after the other in the same location.

Preparing for your meeting is very important. Make sure you do not end up being late and ensure that you are dressed well, as your prospects will judge you the first time they meet you in person. Subconsciously, prospects will likely perceive that a well-dressed person who takes care of him- or herself will take care of them too.

Never show up for a meeting unprepared. Proper preparation prevents poor performance. Take several business cards, working pens, a clean writing pad, your product brochure, terms and conditions of your product, and an order form. If you are selling an information product, a brochure will make your product more tangible and real for your prospect. A great strategy is to create a brochure and deliver that to your prospect before you actually create your product or service. This way, you will find out if your idea has interest without spending time and money in creating it.

To help the meeting feel like a consultation rather than a sales pitch, structure it as follows:

- Start with something positive that isn't related to your business or products
- Ask questions and remain quiet to learn more about your prospects and their problems (remember the 70–30% principle)
- Repeat your prospect's issue to demonstrate you have listened to what they are feeling, for example, 'Okay, so you are not able to (fill in blank) because…'
- Pitch your product or service to solve their problems, as your prospects don't care about you or your product; they care about themselves
- Close – ask for their business or set up another meeting

A great way to ask for prospects' business is to ask, 'So when would you like to start?' or 'The next step would be to fill out the order form.' If they do not feel ready to buy, say, 'How about we set up another meeting further down the line?'

One thing I have discovered is that people buy to solve their problems. For example, when someone buys a power drill, they want the solution that the drill provides. People don't need a Rolex to tell the time, they want the feeling of accomplishment, success and achievement such a watch provides. So think about what you are really selling to your prospect. What do they want, not what do they need? What solution are you giving them to solve their problem? By asking the questions highlighted above, you will get an indication of what that may be.

But how do you actually ask for your prospect's business?

Closing the sale

Closing the sale is asking your prospect for their business, and this is the part where you get the exchange of value – your prospect's money for your product or service. There are some ground rules when it comes to closing the sale.

Highlight their want. Having asked your prospect questions and listened to their answers, you can now highlight the problem that needs solving which is causing them pain.

Remain positive even after closing the sale, no matter how your prospect responds. If the prospect is negative and you are negative too, there is only one outcome.

Stay confident when you are closing the sale. Confidence will make the prospect feel that they are making the right decision in buying your product or service. A great way to create confidence is to know your product inside out as well as understand your customer's problems, wants and needs. Eye contact is key.

Present your proposal in writing. This is one of the reasons why you should always take your brochure, terms and conditions, and order form to meetings. They will show your prospect what they will get once they decide to do business with you. People do not believe what they hear; people believe what they see.

Stay seated while you close a sale, even if your prospect is standing up and walking around. Typically your prospect will also take a seat. When you stand up, you are giving your prospect the indication that the conversation has changed. You don't want to do this when you are closing.

Communicate well. As a police officer, have you ever felt a suspect isn't communicating clearly? Something just feels 'off' and your police officer senses start tingling. That's how your prospect will feel if you do not communicate well during the closing phase. Make sure that you practise the entire structure and closing phase of the meeting. You can record yourself on your phone, audio or video, then play it back to see if you are coming across the way you intend to.

If you cover all these points then your chances of closing the sale are dramatically increased. But you still need to close the sale. There are numerous closing strategies, too many to list in this book, but the most important thing is to ask for your prospect's business. If you do not ask the prospect for their commitment to part with their money, they won't.

A few examples of how to do this are as follows:

- So, when would you like to start?
- Have you seen enough to make a decision?
- After our discussion, I feel as though we have covered everything. How would you like to pay?
- How soon would you like to start benefiting from (your product or service)?

A great way to test the water to find out if your prospect is ready to buy is to give them two options. Either choice advances the sale. Here are a few examples:

- Mr Smith, which delivery date would be better for you, A or B?
- Mrs Jones, will you be the one trained to use the new module, or will you want someone else to be involved?
- Mr Saint, do you want access to the training on Monday or Tuesday?

Don't let fear of sales keep you from selling a product or service your customer is willing to buy. You will be making their life better by doing so, and in actual fact it's a disservice to your prospect if you do not ask. It's your confidence in the product that will help the sale – or at least persuade the customer to consider your business in the future.

If you want further help, why not use some sales tactics.

Using sales tactics

Here are some tactics that I believe will help you sell your product or service to your prospect. Adopt these into your sales strategy and they will increase your closing rate.

Don't mix. Top sales people do not mix their activities. If you are selling your product nine to five, Monday to Friday, ensure that time is used for selling only. Other time can be used for other areas of your business. Be consistent and make your day productive.

Sell with questions, not answers. Your prospect does not care about you, your product or service. They care about themselves and couldn't give a damn if you make the sale or not. Ask questions and listen to their concerns, problems and pain points.

Don't practise in front of your prospect. Practise your new sales presentation behind closed doors. Remember to be prepared for your prospect. They will sniff out if you are not prepared.

First dates. I do not mean take your prospects on a date; I mean get curious about them. On a first date, you wouldn't just talk about yourself and how good you are, would you? You would remain curious about your date. This is the way to act when you are with your prospect. Ask questions about products and services they are already using. Is what they're using now too expensive; not reliable enough; too slow? Find what your customers really need. When you learn what your customers need, you'll find them trusting you as a valued consultant and wanting to do more business with you as a result.

Cultivate a support group. If you want to become a successful entrepreneur, ensure you learn from people who are on the same mission as you. Network with other entrepreneurs and find out what they do to become successful. Attend business programmes and seminars that will help you level up your skillset. The more you learn, the more you earn.

Don't ramble. At the beginning stages of selling your product or service, you will likely have a combination of excitement and nervousness. When this happens, do not ramble on about things that have nothing to do with responding to what your prospect has said.

Keep a journal. It's highly important that you track, record and review your progress at the end of each day. Describe how you met your goals for the day; how many meetings you attended; how many appointments you set. This will prepare you for the next opportunity and enable you to become better in the process.

Use a selling system. To win business and make sales, especially at the beginning stages of your entrepreneurial journey, use a system. There are many selling systems that have great success. Study them and commit to practising them. Once you are generating enough revenue, you can then decide whether to expand and invest in a sales manager for your company.

The golden rule. I first came across this from the highly successful entrepreneur Brian Tracy. The golden rule in selling is to sell with the same honesty, integrity, understanding, empathy and thoughtfulness that you would want if someone was selling to you. As police officers, you likely already use this golden rule, so adapting it for sales will be easy.

Mind-strong. Get mentally and emotionally tough in sales, and in business in general. You may hear more 'nos' than 'yeses', and you need to maintain a healthy sense of self-esteem. When you feel good about yourself, you will work more effectively. Do not take rejections personally. Learn from them and find that yes.

Summary

By now you should understand that selling in your business is vital for its success and growth. We have covered the need to understand your prospect in relation to sales, to listen to your prospect effectively to ensure you're maximising your chances of securing the sale, to ask for your prospect's business by closing the sale, and the various tactics to help you get the best result when it comes to sales.

Having a strong mindset is so important when you are committing yourself to success as an entrepreneur. In fact, it isn't just important, it's essential. The next part of the book, called 'Entrepreneur Essentials', will cover mindset, energy and execution.

Success story – Lorna Reeves

Lorna worked for the Metropolitan Police for fifteen years, but unfortunately her wellbeing suffered because of the stressful working environment. Due to the pressure, her weight fluctuated, she was sleep-deprived, she started to develop stress eczema, ultimately leading to incontinence.

Lorna decided that there was more to her life than the police service. She started a side business baking birthday cakes, but she quickly realised she didn't know how to run or grow a business. Because of this, Lorna attended a Success QuickStart Day. Soon afterwards, she joined the Shifts to Success Accelerator.

Lorna has since stopped baking cakes and is now the founder of MyOhMy Weddings & Events. Her business has thrived, and she has:

- Made weddings sales of £5,000
- Secured contracts worth £17,000 for events
- Won national wedding awards
- Co-authored a best-selling book
- Beaten her previous salary, now earning above £60,000
- Paid off thousands of pounds of debt to become debt-free

I asked Lorna how her life has changed:

Shifts to Success has impacted me on so many levels. The straightforward and deep understanding I gained as part of the course has made the business-building path clear.

By trusting the process and doing the work, I made sure my business would be set up well, be set to scale and represent me and my values. The support and guidance from the mentors has been phenomenal, their desire to see me succeed is almost as strong as my own. Having instant access to various resources is another golden element of the course. Without them I'd still be stuck.

My health, both mental and physical, is 100 times better than it was in the police. In fact, my mindset has shifted to another level. I no longer feel bound to a salary, either; I am free!

PART 3

Entrepreneur Essentials

Chapter 10

Mindset

'The only thing standing between you and your goal is the bullshit story you keep telling yourself as to why you can't achieve it.'

Jordan Belfort

Key learning points:

- Fear is not real
- Reframing risk
- Sacrificing short-term for long-term gain
- Believe that you will succeed
- Failure is not final

Fear is not real

I have some good news and some bad news. The bad news is that fear will be with you for the rest of your life. The good news is that you have the choice whether to let fear control your life or not.

Fear is an emotional mechanism to keep us safe from something that the mind deems risky or uncomfortable. This safety mechanism has been a part of the human mind since day one when it protected us from dangerous animals and hostile tribes. Now it's our subconscious mind's attempt to shield us from risky and harmful situations, including situations that may affect our ego.

Starting any type of business can seem scary. As a beginner, you cannot precisely know the amount of risk involved. Your mind is likely to amplify the potential risk of failures that haven't even happened yet. If you read statistics that say the majority of businesses fail, your mind will automatically think you will be in that majority. This is normal. Everyone has doubts about their abilities.

However, fear is not real. It only exists in our minds. It is a product of our imagination, causing us to fear things that do not currently exist and may never exist. Pretty insane, if you ask me. Fear imprisons us, keeping us from living an extraordinary life.

You have two choices – you can live your fears or live your life. What you fear most is usually what you need to be doing. Once you face that fear, you will likely realise that it was all in your head in the first place.

When I first started in business, I wanted things to go perfectly smoothly, but I came to realise this was never going to happen. I made some mistakes along the way, and I am sure you will too. Personally, now I love fear, because I know the power it can give an individual when they face it and take a step closer to the person they truly want to become.

There are three types of pain that we fear in our lives. Once we understand each one, we can then dissolve them. The first is 'loss pain'.

When we decide to change our lives, we can get fearful of losing something that we like or love. Examples could be losing our job, our spouse, our relationship with our kids, or some sort of benefit. As a police officer, you may be fearful of losing the feeling of security you have. You may be fearful of losing the steady wage coming in each month, the predictability of your career path, supervisors to consult when you need guidance in the job, the camaraderie with colleagues, or even your identity as a police officer. A way to shift your mindset is instead of focusing on the fear of loss, focus on things you are going to gain. For example, you may lose the feeling of security, but you will gain more freedom in your life. You may lose the steady wage, but you could gain a truly rewarding income that doesn't require you to work forty hours a week. You may lose your identity as a police officer, but you will gain a reputation as a successful entrepreneur who supports and helps people throughout the world.

By focusing on what you will gain rather than lose in your life, you will break down those fearful barriers that stop you from taking action.

The second type of fear is called 'growing pain'. This is the fear of change and doing something new and challenging. When I started my own business, I was afraid it was going to be too hard for me to handle, I was afraid I didn't have any competency or knowledge, and I was afraid that I was going to have to work hard every hour of the day without any support. As a police officer, you may be fearful of similar things.

Shift your mindset. Life in general will be challenging. To

grow to new heights in your life, finances, business, health and relationships, you will always go through challenging times. Facing difficulties is what develops us as humans. So instead of looking at a challenge as a negative, look at it as an opportunity to grow your mindset. As Tony Robbins states, 'Life doesn't happen to you, it happens for you.'

Life is a gift, and that includes the challenging times we go through. I don't know If I would be the same person writing this very book if I hadn't gone through depression and wanting to take my own life at the age of twenty-one. At the time it certainly didn't look like an opportunity as it was the lowest point of my life, but thankfully I used that adversity to my advantage.

The third type of fear is called 'results pain'. What if you struggle and work hard to make changes in your life and the grass isn't greener on the other side? The outcome isn't any better than it was at the beginning. You may have fears of not 'making it' and that is normal, but remember you are not quitting your job. You can make the transition to business while still in the police service, so if you do decide to quit on your goals and dreams, you still have your job available to you.

You may be fearful about your lack of experience, expertise or ability in business. Why would anyone listen to you? Why would anyone help you? Why would anyone pay you? You may simply be thinking, 'I am not good enough.' However, the truth is you do not need to be an 'expert' with years of experience to start turning your skills and ideas into money. You just need to be willing to learn and take action.

A powerful mindset shift you can make is to imagine developing a business or life where the grass is greener. I firmly believe that thoughts become things, and if you think of a lifestyle and business that would give you the happiness and fulfilment you want, your mind will get to work on ensuring you put in the work to make it a reality.

These three types of fear are all 'What ifs?' The more you focus on them, the more your mindset will become fixed, which will keep you from taking any action. Stop allowing the 'What if?' fears from preventing you doing the very things that will improve your life.

Reframing risk

Are you willing to die for your job as a police officer? Seriously, if you are not, you need a reality check. Due to the nature of the job, a police officer is always at risk of getting seriously injured or killed.

However, being killed is just one element of risk a police officer faces. So if you don't fear dying as a police officer, what else can life threaten you with? Living on your own terms as a successful entrepreneur? You should laugh in the face of that risk!

Life is all risky. Falling in love is risky; marriage is risky; having children is risky; investing your money is risky. Business is risky, but the worst risk of all is not living a life you desire, because I believe you only get one chance at this thing called life.

In order to have a sense of fulfilment in your life, get out of your comfort zone and take a risk. Once you do, you will expand your whole life and get more out of it.

'To laugh is to risk appearing the fool, to weep is appearing sentimental, to reach out for another is to risk involvement, to expose feelings is to risk exposing your true self, to place your ideas and dreams before a crowd is to risk their loss, to love is to risk not being loved in return, to live is to risk dying, to hope is to risk despair, to try is to risk failure, but risk must be taken, because the greatest hazard in life is to risk nothing. The person who risks nothing, does nothing, has nothing, is nothing. They may avoid suffering and sorrow, but they cannot learn, feel, change, grow, love and live. They are a slave and forfeit their freedom. Only a person who risks is free. '

Les Brown

Regret is an awful thing to experience, especially when you cannot do anything about it. I do not wish it upon anyone. Don't look back on your life and wish you'd had more time; utilise the time you have now to ensure you do not live with regret. Regret weighs tonnes, commitment weighs grammes. Every successful person has jumped, and if you want to become successful, you must jump too. Your parachute will not open right away, and that is normal, but eventually it will, and when it does your life will never be the same. Remember, nothing great was ever achieved in comfort zones, so get comfortable with being uncomfortable. Face your fears and do it anyway.

Sacrificing short-term gain for long-term gain

If you want to become successful, give up on the idea of instant gratification and embrace delayed gratification. In other words, instead of thinking short-term, think long-term.

I hear so many people say they want to become successful, but their actions state otherwise. All they do is consume instead of create. They spend two precious resources that could be better utilised in changing their life for good – time and money. The big difference between the successful and the unsuccessful is how they use those resources.

A creation mindset thinks and acts towards creating things of value to serve people. As an entrepreneur, this will ultimately give you the lifestyle you want. Successful people throughout the world come from a creation mindset. They sacrifice the things that come from a consumption mindset.

People think it is normal to watch TV, go away on holiday each year and buy things. However, successful people understand they can do all that when they reach their goals. In the early stages, they sacrifice those things for the betterment of their lives.

A friend of mine, who used to insist on having at least three holidays a year, focused on building her business with her partner. She sacrificed her holidays for a year and used her valued resources, time and money to build a life where she wouldn't need to 'escape' any more. Her income from her business now far exceeds her job salary, and she expects to leave her job completely in the coming months. She is extremely happy that she sacrificed her holidays for a year so she never has to work in a job again.

If you want to change your life and become your own boss outside the police service, you will have to sacrifice a fair amount of your rest days and annual leave. The more work you put into your business, the faster you will have the opportunity to leave the police service. Your life can change within a year if you put your business first.

How many business books have you read in the last year? How many seminars or workshops have you attended? How many new skills have you acquired or developed? How many investments have you made in yourself that could alter your life in a positive way?

In the last year, how many parties have you attended? How many holidays have you been on? How many hours of TV and films have you watched? How many times have you been to the local pub? How many hours have you aimlessly trawled through the internet? How many times have you bought something that you don't really need? If the answers to the second set of questions far exceed the answers to the first, that is where you are going wrong. If what you are doing right now isn't working, heed the advice of someone who has successfully done what you want to do. That is exactly what I did.

I chose delayed gratification over instant gratification, and now I can choose how to spend my time. We all have twenty-four hours in a day; it's how we use those hours that separates the successful from the unsuccessful.

Next time you are making the decision to buy something, ask yourself whether the money could be used to help you change your life. Next time you decide to watch TV or party with friends, ask yourself whether you could use the time to learn about business, wealth creation and entrepreneurship instead. You only have to sacrifice these things while you are building a business. Once you have the success you want, you can travel more, have lie-ins, watch TV, and go to parties. But I have a funny feeling that when you reach success, a creation mindset will be at your core and you will continue to choose delayed gratification over instant gratification.

Believe that you will succeed

If you do not believe you can achieve amazing things in your life, you won't. If you believe a certain thing about yourself, you actually embody that belief. Being successful in life is about having the proper belief system that you have what it takes. There is a great quote by Henry Ford, 'Whether you think you can or you think you can't – you're right.' Belief is critical.

When you believe in your ability to achieve incredible success in your life beyond the police force, your actions drive that belief. As a result, massive *shifts to success* will happen (see what I did there?). Your tone of voice will be different, your confidence will rise, you will walk with an upbeat gait and you will generally feel good about yourself. By believing that you can achieve whatever you want out of your life, you give your brain the proper wiring it needs to bring those things to fruition.

Before May 1954, the universal belief was that a human was not physically capable of running a four-minute mile. It had been tried numerous times, but people had always failed. However, there was one man who did believe it could be done.

His name was Roger Bannister, and he broke that four-minute mile barrier for the first time in history. Since then, people from all over the world have also broken the four-minute mile.

What had changed? People's belief systems had changed. They knew that the challenge could be done. They knew that what had once seemed impossible was now possible.

That is what I want you to do – change your belief system. If someone else's dreams can become a reality, so can yours. Sometimes people need to see someone else do it before they can do it themselves. How could I, a man from a broken family who was financially broke, had no business experience, was an average student at school, end up creating a six figure business, owning over a million pounds' worth of assets, and becoming a speaker, business coach, mentor and author? It was because I believed I could do it. You too can achieve success beyond the police force.

I hear, 'Be realistic,' all the time, generally from those who do not believe in themselves. By incorporating that statement into their belief system, they will carry on along the road to mediocrity for the rest of their lives. Why not believe in yourself to achieve big things?

I believe that we are who we choose to be. I chose success as an entrepreneur to provide me with freedom. Believe in yourself. You are capable of achieving great things in your lifetime, but only if you first believe you can.

Failure is not final

On your path as an entrepreneur, you will experience failure. A lot of people think that they won't reach the successful life they want as an entrepreneur because they have failed. However, this is not the case. People who do not become successful simply give up and quit.

It is never the failure that stops us, but most people do stop at their first failure. Every successful entrepreneur I have spoken to and studied over the past six years has a common trait and this is that they do not stop because they have hit one failure, ten failures, one hundred failures or even one thousand failures. They commit to their goals and affirm to themselves that they will do whatever it takes to achieve them.

Think about a child learning how to ride a bike. They topple over, scrape their knees, then jump back on to attempt to ride the bike again. Despite failing over and over, they push on and finally achieve their goal.

We are supposed to fail. Success is never linear, and I personally have failed loads of times. I remember when I was building my first company, I missed out on a great investment opportunity that would have generated thousands of pounds each year for a lifetime.

When I explained this to one of my mentors, Simon Zutshi, he looked at me in the eye and said, 'Alex, don't fuck about, be quicker!' That was all I needed. That feedback ensured I was always the first one to make an offer to secure a deal, which really helped change my results.

I look at a failure as a stepping stone to success. Each stone is an opportunity to gain wisdom. It is how we react to failure that determines our outcome in life. When I coach and mentor people in business and they tell me how they have failed, I congratulate them because that tells me they are working. They are trying and becoming better in the process.

You will not fully appreciate success without failure, as failure makes achieving success taste all the sweeter. You will stumble, fall, hit obstacles, get rejected, not hit targets, but armed with your entrepreneurial compass, you will arrive at your goal. It may take a year, it may take two years, or five years, but you will succeed as long as you keep going, learning from each failure you encounter.

There is an incredible true story I want to share with you about a man you may have heard of. He lost his father at the age of five. At sixteen, he quit school, and by seventeen he had already lost four jobs. He joined the army and failed. He applied for law school and was rejected. He became an insurance salesman and failed again. At the age of nineteen he became a father, and by the time he was twenty his wife had left him and taken their baby daughter. He then failed in an attempt to kidnap his own daughter.

At the age of sixty-five, he retired and received a cheque from the government for $105. He decided to commit suicide because he thought life wasn't worth living any more as he had failed so much. As he sat under a tree to write his will, instead he wrote what he could have accomplished with his life. There was much that he hadn't yet done, and he realised the one thing he could do better than anyone he knew was cook.

He borrowed $87 against his cheque and bought some chicken. Frying it up using his own recipe, he then went door to door to sell it to his neighbours in Kentucky. By the age of eighty-eight, Colonel Sanders, founder of the Kentucky Fried Chicken (KFC) empire, was a billionaire.

I hope you become financially independent and successful much sooner than Colonel Sanders, but his story drives home the point. True failure in life is when you decide to quit or not even try at all. By continually failing and learning, you will succeed. It's just a matter of time. So embrace failure and welcome it. It isn't final.

Summary

Having a strong mindset is crucial for success, but do not worry if you feel as though you don't have one yet. Typically, your mindset will get shaped on your entrepreneurial journey. Fear will always be a part of your life, but you can shift your mindset from letting fear control you to you controlling fear. Life will always be risky, especially when you're a police officer, so you may as well take a risk and build a life you desire.

To reach success, you are going to have to sacrifice some things for the time being, but once you have achieved your goals, you can go back to those things if you so please. Cultivate your belief system and realise that failure is a normal process, then you will continually learn and keep on going towards success.

In the next chapter, I will cover the second 'entrepreneur essential' for success, Energy.

Chapter 11

Energy

'Energy and persistence conquer all things.'

Benjamin Franklin

Key learning points:

- Getting the energy drainers out of your life
- Effort drives momentum
- Motivational strategies to stay energetic
- Work-life balance

Getting the energy drainers out of your life

When you decide to change your life for the better, you will more than likely get someone criticising your decision. This criticism could come from friends, family or the general public. You may get called antisocial, an introvert, or boring – I had them all, and a lot worse. But what these critics fail to realise is that you are creating a lifestyle they don't have the balls to create.

Once I was having a conversation with a good friend and colleague about going into business while we were working in custody. Another colleague overheard my plans and said in a patronising manner, 'Oh, we are working with millionaires now, are we?' This was totally uncalled for and it hurt me. Even writing this now brings back the feeling of hurt I had many years ago. I didn't react, but I made a promise to myself that I would prove that colleague's cynicism wrong. Two years on, I have done just that and become financially independent.

Shut out these negative comments. When people say these things it is generally because they feel insecure about what you are trying to create. They want to keep you down on their level and change your mindset to their way of thinking. Remain focused and cut out that noise.

Another term for energy drainers is 'crabs'. If you were to put a single crab in a bucket, that crab would climb out and escape. However, if you place a group of crabs in a bucket and one single crab decides to escape, the other crabs will gang up and pull it back down. If the crab persists, unfortunately the other crabs will ultimately kill it.

Although energy drainers won't kill you, they do have a similar mentality. If you want to achieve success and better your circumstances to escape your current environment, there will be people (crabs) who will try and pull you back.

Celebrities, athletes, politicians and other successful entrepreneurs all have haters and energy drainers, so you are not alone. There are a lot of people who will support you and want to see you succeed, and you will be attracted to and associate with these people more and more as you do so.

I interviewed millionaire entrepreneur and best-selling author Simon Zutshi and asked him about the importance of peer groups. He explained that if you want to become better in life, you need to surround yourself with people who are better than you in a certain area, as they will force you to up your own game to match theirs. And it is totally true.

Jim Rohn says, 'You're the average of the five people you spend the most time with.' We are greatly influenced by those closest to us. They affect our way of thinking, our self-esteem, and our decisions. Of course, everyone is their own person, but research has shown that we're affected by our environment. This is why it is so important to have mentors and coaches to guide you.

Haters and energy drainers are a sign that you are doing something great in your life. You are working hard and pushing yourself to the limit. So when you start getting haters or energy drainers, look at that as success giving you a little wink and saying, 'You are on the right path, keep going.' And that is exactly what you should do – keep on going, regardless of some people's reactions and criticism.

Effort drives momentum

Effort drives momentum, which in turn increases your energy as an entrepreneur. Many people think that putting effort into something will zap their energy, but this isn't the case. The more effort you put in, the quicker you build momentum and results. When this happens, you will look back at all the progress you have made and almost certainly not want to lose the momentum you have gained.

A major part of any success is your work ethic, which correlates to the amount of effort you put into your goals. You don't have to be the smartest, quickest or wealthiest person when you start off in business, but one thing you do need is the ability to put in the effort. The difference between the ordinary and the extraordinary is doing that little bit extra.

I personally think it is a bad thing when school teachers and organisations reward children or participants who come third, fourth, fifth and so on. They basically reward people for taking part. But life isn't like that. The market, your competition, your customers won't reward you with success for taking part. They reward those who put in consistent effort.

Winners in life leave it all on the table, and when the going gets hard, they keep pushing through. Success is not just given, it is earned and deserved by those people who grind it out, no matter what the circumstance. They could be working forty hours a week in their full-time jobs, but they still work on their side hustle business regardless of how tired they are.

One of the things we can control in life is our work ethic. If you can't look at yourself in the mirror at the end of each day and tell yourself you have given your all to change your and your family's lives for the better, you don't deserve success. However, if you have, regardless of whether you have hit a goal or not, you have succeeded. Success doesn't always lie in your results, but in your effort. Doing your best is all that matters.

I once watched an amazing interview with an ex-Navy

SEAL called David Goggins who spoke about the 40% Rule. When your mind whispers to you, 'You have done enough for today', 'Relax, you will get burned out', 'You have done all you can' and so on, you are really only 40% done. What a kick in the teeth! However, this is a great way of pushing past what you think is enough, thereby increasing your effort to reach your goals as a successful entrepreneur. There is no easy way to success, otherwise everyone would be financially independent, have fabulous bodies, and be driving flashy cars or travelling across the globe.

We all have a reserve tank, so when that little voice in your mind whispers, 'You have done enough,' it is time to access that reserve tank and put more effort in. Once you tap into your reserve tank, you will likely find a new sense of energy and appreciation for your work ethic, and because of this you will put even more effort in. An added benefit of the 40% Rule is that it can be used in different areas of your life – business, health and fitness, relationships, finance or personal development.

If you could buy success from a shop, the price tag wouldn't be in monetary terms. It would be in terms of effort. Effort is the trade-off – you must give up something in order to get something. But the rewards and fulfilment that come from true success are well worth the effort and fight. Success is never owned, it is only rented, and the rent is due every single day. That is what successful entrepreneurs do – they give maximum effort every day of their lives, even when they don't feel like it.

You will have different outcomes in your life and business, there is no doubting that. There will be times when amazing things happen that make you feel euphoric, and there will be times when absolutely awful things will happen, but know that you can get a grip on the outcome through your own effort.

Motivational strategies to stay energetic

If you are motivated by this book, unfortunately that will not last forever, as motivation never does. Motivation can only get you going. I use motivation in different ways, and I will share some with you.

I review my goals every single morning and night. This helps me stay motivated and reminds me what I am working towards.

Generally, we write down our goals to better ourselves. When we write them initially, we are full of motivation and energy, but as always, the motivation will fade sooner or later. However, by reviewing my goals, I recreate that spark, which motivates me to keep up the energy in working towards achieving them.

Another way to motivate yourself through your goals is to set three for each day. When you achieve them, no matter how big or small they are, they will motivate you because you have made more progress towards your ultimate life-changing goals.

I set rewards for myself. If I know I have achieved something great for my business, hit a milestone or a goal, I will reward myself. For example, when I reached an income of £62,000 p.a. from my first business, I booked a holiday in Barcelona for me and my partner at the time. While writing this book, I would have a play with my dog, Rolo, or grab a coffee each time I hit the next 3,000 words. Another reward could be a social event with friends, such as a meal out with a few drinks.

It's important that you treat yourself from time to time when you are building a business as the reward gives pleasure to your brain and reinforces why you are doing the work in the first place. This creates further motivation and energy.

I consume motivational content. I go on to YouTube and watch inspiring and impactful videos by highly successful entrepreneurs. I also listen to great podcasts such as 'School of Greatness' by Lewis Howes and the Dent podcast by Glen Carlson. This activity really fires me up, and I hope that it does the same for you. Most successful people overcame some adversity in their life to start off on their entrepreneurial journey, which shows what is possible for you too.

I use my purpose. When I first became financially independent, I vividly remember sitting down on my partner's mother's sofa and thinking about what I had achieved. I had gone from nothing to owning many cash flowing assets, having joint ventures with two incredible business partners, being featured in business and investment magazines and interviewed for podcast shows, and getting invited to speak at business events around the UK. Life was great. I could have retired at twenty-six and never had to work in a job again.

But something was wrong internally. My partner at the time came in and asked, 'What's wrong?' wrapping her arms around me tightly. I explained to her that I didn't know. I just felt empty. That empty feeling stayed with me for a few days, and then it hit me. I had climbed the entrepreneurial ladder of success, and once I reached the top, I realised that my ladder was leaning against the wrong building.

There is an awesome quote by Tony Robbins: 'Success without fulfilment is the ultimate failure.' Although I wouldn't say it was the ultimate failure for me, it was, however, a big wake-up call. It gave me a boost of motivation and energy to search for what would fulfil me. The hunt was on.

When I asked myself, 'Alex, what will fulfil you? What do you love?' I couldn't find the answer at all and this really pissed me off. To help me with this, I bought a small journal so I could write down all the business ideas that popped into my head. I didn't care if they were bad business ideas or not, they went in my journal.

I carried my journal everywhere for months, and about six months in, I had filled half of it with my brain dump ideas. Now, I must be honest, the ideas in my journal were not particularly good – in fact, who am I kidding? They were shit. I would read the pages, flicking through them, frustratingly saying, 'No, no, no, God no!' Nothing really jumped out at me.

But then something strange happened. I noticed there was a common theme on every single page.

I grabbed a highlighter pen and highlighted these common themes. Every business idea contained the following:

- Successful people
- Helping people become successful
- Entrepreneurship
- Personal development
- Motivating people
- Inspiring people

- Helping people become wealthier
- Helping prime people's mindset for success
- Public speaking
- Online business

My conscious mind was so fixed on finding out what interested me, what excited and what would fulfil me, it was just dumping awful ideas. But my subconscious mind, which is the more powerful of the two minds, was screaming loud and clear what I should be focusing on. When I connected these dots, I had the most euphoric feeling as I knew what would fulfil me.

What I did was focus only on business ideas that aligned with the highlighted common themes, my purpose. It didn't take me long to launch an interview-based brand called Ultra-Preneur®. I would travel around the UK, interviewing highly successful entrepreneurs on their mindset, business, wealth, stories and personal development in the hope it would inspire and motivate people into changing their lives to become successful entrepreneurs. If you are interested in watching these interviews, you can still find them on YouTube.

I really loved what I was doing and I wasn't even producing a profit from it. Not exactly a good business model, but at that time I didn't care.

After an amazing interview with entrepreneur, speaker and best-selling author Daniel Priestley, who is the co-founder of an incredible company called Dent, a lightbulb popped on in my head. With Daniel's help I had found my niche – to help police officers, my ex-colleagues, who wanted a different career path beyond the police force.

My purpose felt stronger than ever. After speaking to

an ex-police officer about PTSD, depression and suicidal thoughts, I wanted to try to give them another opportunity in life and prevent this from happening to other police officers. Thus Shifts to Success was born, and the energy I have for this business is like nothing I have ever felt before. My purpose, my personal mission, is to help 100 police officers build successful businesses by 2020, while contributing to charities that support police officers suffering from depression and PTSD. My big vision is to help police officers globally.

Finding your purpose will take a little work. If you are a police officer who knows there is other work out there for you to do that will serve people in an impactful way, listen to those thoughts. If you do, you will find a new type of energy that never depletes.

Work–life balance

I am going to let you into a huge secret on how to find work–life balance…

You don't need to!

I don't want to give you any fluff. When it comes to your business goals, I'm sorry to say, work–life balance is bullshit. You will hear from people, 'Slow down'; 'Have a break'; 'You've got to have balance, you know'. But I would disagree with these comments. Do you think Elon Musk had balance? Do you think Michael Jordan or Serena Williams had balance in their lives? What about Tiger Woods? Or Steve Jobs? What about Grant Cardone, Arnold Schwarzenegger, Oprah Winfrey, Gary Vaynerchuk or Sara Blakely? The list could go on.

If you want to achieve great things in your life, whatever that greatness may be for you, there is going to have to be an imbalance for you to achieve those things. You are going to have to give your business priority. If you try and find work-life balance, all that you will end up doing is juggling several things at once. This in turn will stop you from making any real progress in anything, meaning you will lose focus.

Let's use an example. If one entrepreneur works twelve hours a week on their business and one works forty hours a week, which one will be more likely to achieve success? The entrepreneur who works forty hours a week on their business; the one with the work-life imbalance.

In my first company, for the first two years, I worked unbelievably hard. I didn't see friends; I cut out going to social events; I cut out date nights, birthdays, the gym, and it paid off. I now have money and freedom because I don't have to work in a job. And now I have more goals I want to achieve, I'm doing the exact same thing again. When I was writing this book, I ensured I wrote every single day for seven weeks straight.

I get that it will be hard. You may have kids and a spouse and all you seem to be doing is working, but ask yourself why you are working on your business in the first place. You are doing the right thing, and the work-life balance will come when you have achieved all you want to achieve. By having an imbalance now, you will have greater balance in the future, because you will have gained freedom from your job.

So remember, great results come from great imbalances, not great work-life balances. Decide what's more important for you: a permanent mediocre balanced life or a temporarily unbalanced life that will provide you with remarkable results. If you choose the latter, I promise you it will be worth it in the end.

Summary

The people you surround yourself with are highly important when you are trying to achieve success. Maybe it is time to have a serious think about your own circle of influence, as people who don't support you will try their best to suck the energy out of you. Surround yourself with winners.

Effort is the driving force behind every accomplishment. When you think you have done enough, you are only really 40% done. Access your energy reserve tank to push past the discomfort and go the extra mile. Motivation will die, so use a resource to help you pick up the energy towards building a fulfilling life.

You can have all the energy in the world, but you will remain in the same position if you don't take massive determined action, which we will cover in the next chapter.

Chapter 12

Execution

'The path to success is to take massive determined action.'

Tony Robbins

Key learning points:

- Procrastination is a killer to success
- Every decision you make matters
- Throw away your excuses
- Hoping is not a strategy to change your life

Procrastination kills success

Has there ever been a time when you knew you should do something, but you kept putting it off for another day? Yep, me too. However, successful people push past procrastination. They do not make up excuses. Procrastination can be beaten, it just takes some self-awareness and effort.

Procrastinators sabotage themselves. They put obstacles in

their own path and tell lies to themselves, such as, 'I'll do this tomorrow, as tomorrow is a better day for me,' or 'I can do this next week because then it will allow me to do that.' But they do not get the urge the next day or next week. Then they try and make themselves feel better by telling themselves, 'This isn't important,' or 'I don't want to do this anyway.'

Another huge lie procrastinators tell themselves is that time pressure makes them more creative. Unfortunately, this is not the case. All they end up doing is wasting precious resources such as time and opportunity.

People who procrastinate will actively look for distractions, normally ones that don't take a lot of commitment such as checking e-mail. These distractions control emotions such as fear of failure. The thing is, if procrastinators never start, they'll never have a chance to fail, but they'll never have a chance to succeed, either.

We can stop ourselves from procrastinating using strategies that successful people use. These strategies are highly effective in pushing us into getting shit done (GSD), which will ultimately progress us towards changing our lives.

A powerful strategy is to make yourself accountable to others. I have personally used this strategy for the past six years and it has never failed me yet. I openly share my goals and intentions with my loved ones, the reasons being

a) I will look and feel like a fool if I don't come through on my word, and
b) I don't want to let my loved ones down.

Create accountability by asking friends or family for a weekly call or daily text. Writing this book, I spoke to a friend every week and she asked for my word count. If I did not make my word count for a particular week, I felt awful. I didn't just feel as though I'd let myself down, I felt I'd let her down too.

If you want to start a business and become a successful entrepreneur, tell people you are going to do just that.

Time blocking is another powerful strategy to beat procrastination. Successful people like to remain organised and focused when they are doing a particular task, and time blocking prevents them from multi-tasking, which is one of the easiest ways to procrastinate. Time blocking is a simple process. All it requires you to do is block time out in your schedule for the task you need to do, and do nothing but the task in that blocked out time. You can start off giving yourself thirty minute time blocks, but I would recommend you build this up the more confident you get at using blocked out time to your full advantage. Apps such as Time Doctor can help, but I would start off by using your smartphone's alarm.

When you have blocked out time for your tasks, ensure you put your smartphone on airplane mode. Your friends and family can live without you for an hour or so. Don't let other people distract you from your agenda, otherwise you will never get anything done.

A great way to avoid people trying to get your attention when you are focused on GSD is to tell them you won't be available at a certain time because you are busy building your business and life towards better things.

It's also important to stop being a yes man or woman. It's quite easy to get sucked into saying yes to everything, but it's our responsibility to use the power of no to our advantage. By doing everything and anything for friends, family, colleagues, etc., we make little room for ourselves, and thus the day gets away, knocking back our tasks and goals.

Work on your tasks first, and only when your tasks are complete reach out and help others. As Warren Buffet says, 'The difference between successful people and really successful people is that really successful people say no to almost everything.'

Our brains get fatigued by the number of decisions we make in a day. Imagine a battery signal. At the start of the day, it's at 100%, but by the end of the day, it's down to 10%. Because of this, it would be wise to get your most important tasks complete in the morning, even if that means waking up an hour earlier than you normally do.

Every decision you make matters

We live in an instant world due to all the technology that is around us, so the majority of people want what they want *now*. People throughout the world are seeking a shortcut to success and the financial freedom that comes with it. But what they fail to realise is that every successful person has gone through a shit load of process. Did Cristiano Ronaldo became the world's best football player by pure luck? What about boxer Floyd Mayweather, retiring with all his riches and a 50–0 winning record? Hell, no. They went through a tough, uncomfortable process that included sacrifices, difficult training and a relentless work ethic behind the scenes.

Successful people know that they must commit to a process which drives progress, which in turn drives momentum, which then turns into the event. Successful events cannot exist without the process. There is no shortcut. If you want to become successful, become your own boss to live your life on your terms, *do not* become event driven. Become process driven. That is the path to success.

Daily decisions affect and alter your life. Success or failure never happens from one huge decision. It happens from small, easy to make decisions that may look insignificant, but done on a consistent basis, over a long period of time, add towards the process.

Is going for a run in the rain an easy decision? Is deciding to become wealthy an easy decision? Is deciding to develop your mindset an easy decision? Yes, they all are. There are only two options: yes or no. Whatever choice you make, it will look insignificant.

Let's look at an example. If I were to eat a pizza right now, I wouldn't be unhealthy tomorrow. If I were to eat the same pizza every day for a week, I'd probably still not be unhealthy. Those decisions to eat a pizza would feel like they didn't matter.

However, if I ate that pizza every single day for a year, that easy daily decision would get serious. I would be overweight, unhealthy, lethargic. My sex drive would be low, my girlfriend may have left me, and I would need medication. Then, lo and behold, I may end up dying fifteen years earlier than I was supposed to do.

Small daily decisions have a cumulative effect on the outcome, the event. The concept of process and event is always working in the background in our lives. Become aware of your daily decisions, which are ultimately going to take you either closer towards your goals or further away from them.

Don't chill on your rest days from the police. Make the decision to consume personal development content; read business books; socialise with entrepreneurs who force you to level up and genuinely want to see you succeed. Manage your money effectively and put away a percentage of your income for business investments, and you will progress towards building a successful business.

When I am faced with small daily decisions, I first recognise that I have a clear vision of the person I want to become in two, three, four, five years' time. Secondly, I ask myself whether the decision is going to take me closer towards that vision I have of myself, or is it going to take me further away? If it is going to take me closer, then I'll generally do it. If it's not, I won't do it. That right there is process and event.

We have two choices in life. We can accept and stick with our current circumstances or we can take the responsibility to change them. Ask yourself which choice you are making each day.

Throw away your excuses

Most people have excuses, and typically they use the same ones over and over again. Your own excuse may be creeping into your mind right now as you think about becoming financially independent as a successful entrepreneur. It's a good idea to face these excuses head on. If you don't, they will keep you working in the police service, clocking on shift, working awful hours for an unrewarding salary.

An excuse is generally a justification for taking or not

taking action on something. When people give themselves an excuse, they do not have full responsibility for their lives. For example, when people are late for an event and blame the traffic, that is a lack of personal responsibility. It isn't the traffic's fault they're late; it's the individual's and only theirs. They could have woken up earlier, been more organised, left home earlier or taken a different route.

Excuses are never reasons. They are false realities to explain why you did or didn't do something, generally to help you feel better about yourself, not look the fool and/or not take ownership of your faults. Making excuses in your life will never change or improve your situation. However, discovering the real issue behind your excuses will.

Think about when you have made an arrest in the past. There is a high probability that the person you arrested made an excuse of some sort, playing the victim. Every person I processed in custody seemed to have an excuse.

Although you are not like the people you arrest in terms of ethics and behaviours, you may have the same kind of mentality in that you do not take personal responsibility for the way your life currently is. This could be a reason why you are not wealthy, not your own boss, not more successful and are unhappy in your job.

Do you make any of the following excuses?

- I don't have the money to build a business
- I don't have the time to build a business
- I have kids and I can't risk going into business
- I am too old to start a business
- I am too young to start a business

- I am not smart enough to become successful
- My spouse/partner doesn't approve of me going into business
- I have to find balance in my life
- I am already overworked so I can't build a business
- I don't have enough business knowledge
- I am in debt so I can't build a business
- I don't like reading too much
- The economy is bad
- I'm tired
- I need a holiday
- I don't feel like working on my goals right now
- Someone else has done my idea
- There is too much competition
- I have too much bad luck

The list could go on and on.

Highlight any excuse you keep using. Now ask yourself, 'Will this excuse make my life or situation any better?' The answer is no. Nothing about excuses will ever move you to a better outcome for your life.

Successful people do not make excuses; they take full and complete ownership of their actions and inactions because they know that there are no justifications for why they did or didn't get a certain outcome. They do not play the victim. They know that things don't just happen to them, things happen *because* of them. This is a huge reason why successful people's lives turn out the way they do.

When I speak at events, the host introduces me. I get clapped on stage and I stand in the centre until the applause has ceased. You can hear a pin drop as the audience waits in anticipation of what I am going to say.

The first thing I say is, 'I am going to need a volunteer.' I then see most of the audience look down so as not to make eye contact with me at this point. After an awkward minute or so, someone raises their hand and I welcome them to join me centre stage. I ask their name, shake their hand, give them £10 and ask them to take their seat once again as the audience and I applaud them.

Of course, £10 is hardly life changing. What is life changing is the action the volunteer took in plucking up the courage to raise their hand. It reinforces the point that if you want to win at life, you have to stop making excuses and take action. Nothing happens until you take action.

When I ask the audience why they didn't take action, I get excuses such as:

- I didn't want to look like an idiot
- I was too far back in the room
- I was afraid that I might do something wrong
- I was waiting for you to tell me more

After gathering all these excuses, I then explain to the audience that they are the same excuses that will prevent them from succeeding in life. There is a universal law in life, which says, 'How you do anything is how you do everything.' If you are holding yourself back in one area, there is a chance you will be holding yourself back in other areas of life, too.

There is no excuse that will ever make you become successful. Having excuses run your life is an indication you have a minimal sense of personal responsibility. When you do stop making excuses and take full responsibility, you can then, and only then, start looking for solutions as to why you haven't got what you want in life. In turn, you will avoid certain situations that prompted you to make the excuse in the first place.

Hoping is not a strategy to change your life

There is a lot of fluff out there about wishing your way to success by visualising it, making affirmations about it and generally wanting it to happen. However, this is all useless if you don't take massive, determined and consistent action. Hoping that you will feel better, become better and live a more rewarding life is not a smart strategy.

The primary difference between winners and losers, the successful and the unsuccessful, is that winners follow through on their goals. They know that action breeds success. As Nike's powerful slogan says, 'Just do it.' Do it and do it and do it until the goal is achieved.

When you decide to act and challenge yourself to get the outcome you truly want for yourself, your life will take on a whole new meaning. It's not about being the smartest, the one with the best idea, the coolest, the best looking, the one with the most cash or time; it's about taking action on a consistent basis towards the goals you have for yourself. Saying, wishing and hoping will never bring them to fruition.

The world doesn't pay you for what you know; it pays you for what you do with what you know. Many people get weighed down by planning, analysing and organising, waiting for the non-existent 'perfect' time, when all they need to do is take massive determined action.

The right action will trigger a series of events that will inevitably carry you to success. It lets those around you know that you are serious about changing your life, which will pique their interest in you. People who are on the same mission as you will become aligned with you and support, encourage and motivate you. You will learn lessons from real life experience that cannot be learnt by reading books and watching the news. You gain clarity on things that were once confusing; things that appeared difficult become easy. Feedback enables you to improve upon your efforts. Take massive determined action and remarkable things will flow in your favour.

Don't be the guy or girl who talks about how 'one day' they will become successful. Talk is cheap without the right action towards goals. It always bewilders me when I catch up on the progress of people I meet on development programmes and discover they haven't taken any steps towards building a better business, but are still saying, 'One day I will.' What I've come to learn is that 'one day' is actually code for 'no day'.

Another bad strategy is to dip your toe into building a business, but not fully immerse yourself in the process. You have to commit to success; you can't say you will try to become successful, because when you try, you are giving yourself an invitation to quit. 'If I fail, it's not my fault. I did try.' You need to change that 'try' to a 'do' or a 'must'.

Say to yourself right now, 'I will try and become successful.' Then say. 'I *must* become successful.' Which is the more powerful statement? Give up the idea of 'trying' and commit to 'doing', because incredible things will happen when you do.

When I speak about action, I get a lot of people asking me, 'Alex, how much action do I need to take?'

I explain to them, 'As much as it takes to succeed.'

Be mindful with action that the more you take, the more likely your chances are of succeeding. There are no shortcuts. There is a reason why you have to take massive action rather than just average action, and that is because average action is a dream killer. It fools people into thinking they are taking action towards their goals, but the reality is they are not taking enough action. They need massive action.

For example, people who read book after book on business, wealth and entrepreneurship will stimulate a sense that they're taking action in the right direction. However, nothing changes. Even though the action of reading business books by successful people is good, it's not *massive* action. Creating a business plan, joining a business programme, conducting market research and picking a niche are all types of massive action.

I can always tell if someone is serious about changing their lives by their actions. If you want to change your life for the better beyond the police force, start taking action right now. Do not wait. There is never a perfect time to start working towards your goals, because something will always pop up that you did not expect. No one is going to do the work for you. The sooner you start, the sooner you can live a life full of freedom, joy, fulfilment and success.

Summary

Procrastination is poison and it will take away your dreams and goals. It will keep you in the police service and living a life of mediocrity. However, by applying the strategies to defeat it, you will be well on your way to turning the ordinary into the extraordinary.

Every single decision you make daily will have a ripple effect towards a positive or negative outcome. Although these daily decisions may seem insignificant on their own, they will always matter. Take personal responsibility and throw out the excuses to regain control of your life.

Everything that you have read in this book is worthless without you taking massive, consistent action towards your dreams and goals. For your life to change, you have to change, and it starts with your actions. You have incredibly valuable skillsets as police officers that can be transferred into the business world as an entrepreneur.

Conclusion

Sometimes you have to go through some shit

Before we finish this book together, I want to share a story on how I came to resign from the police service. The day I decided to resign was the worst day in my career to date...

I had just clocked on to work a twelve hour Friday night shift. As always, there was a long queue of police officers with their detainees at the main custody desk, waiting to get served by the custody sergeants or detention officers. The majority of the time it was a noisy environment, and Friday night wasn't the best of shifts.

On this particular shift, one of my sergeants shouted, 'Alex, I need you.'

'What's wrong?' I asked. He explained that a detainee in the cells had wrapped his jacket around his neck.

As I approached the cell with my custody sergeant, a foul smell hit me like a ton of bricks. I knew what was coming, but I really did not want to admit it to myself. My sergeant opened the door and ... let's just say that what followed wasn't pleasant. I came away from the cell in urgent need of a shower. My partner at the time normally kissed me when I walked through the door, but, despite my frantic attempts to wash myself in the locker room before leaving the station, she passed on this occasion. I jumped in the shower, pouring shower gel all over my body, scrubbing like a madman. I was so demoralised about what had just happened, and paranoid in case I had caught some kind of disease.

Then, relief washed over me. It was like a light bulb went on in my mind.

'Alex, why are you still working there?' I asked myself.

Thankfully, by that time my business was doing pretty well and I was producing great profit. I had the choice to resign and still live a great life. In fact, the quality of my life would improve.

When I got out of the shower, I had a brief chat with Claire and we both agreed that it was time for me to resign from the police service. The next shift, I handed in my notice to my inspector, and let me tell you how that felt. Awesome! I was now free from working in a job. I was completely free. I was an entrepreneur.

I asked Steven Thompson, ex-police officer and Founder of BIGDaddy PR, how he felt when he handed in his notice of resignation.

During the ten months leading up to my resignation, I was concerned. However, I had a sense of a higher purpose which was supporting me and driving me. I've since been able to develop into a better, healthier person, mentally and physically, and I'm free on a much higher level.

I also asked ex-police officer turned successful entrepreneur Rick Gannon how it felt for him handing in his notice. He explained he did something different.

I initially took a career break for eighteen months. It was a little daunting, but I knew I would never achieve my goals in the police. Leaving the force has had a positive effect on my mindset. I now spend precious time with my family and don't have to work after 2.30pm, plus I have every weekend off.

What I have come to realise is that we all go through shit in our lives – metaphorically for most people, and in my case, the real deal, too – from the day my dad left home to the moments when I was at my lowest, wanting to kill myself. I've gone through bad times, but it's those bad times that made me stronger. We have to go through the bad to get to the good. So if you are experiencing a bad time in your life right now, whether it's debt, relationship issues, the job or other personal issues, the good times are coming, I promise, if you take control and start designing the life you truly want.

When I now look back on that smelly night shift, it reminds me of the amazing film *Shawshank Redemption*, where Andy Dufresne, the lead character, has to crawl through a sewer full of shit to escape from prison. Once he gets out, he removes his t-shirt, looks up to the rainy night sky and raises his arms in bliss, knowing he has achieved his freedom.

Your current job as a police officer may feel like a prison. If you could have any wish granted, would it be to work in the police service for the rest of your career? If yes, that is great and I am sincerely happy for you. If not, your soul is telling you there is some other meaningful work in the world for you to do. Work that you *choose* to do as an entrepreneur.

I am not anti-police; I am pro-options and pro-you. We need the police service, and I have nothing but gratitude and respect for police officers across the world. But I encourage those officers who want more out of life beyond the police force to take the first step. Decide in this moment that your life will never be the same again; that you will succeed.

Being an entrepreneur isn't an extraordinary phenomenon. All business skills call be learnt, so don't doubt yourself. Entrepreneurs are never born; they are made. I believe you have an entrepreneur within you ready to break out, so make the change and live your life.

Next steps

If you are a serving or ex-police officer thinking about building your own business – or maybe you already have a business and would like to scale – I would encourage you to go to www. shiftstosuccess.com/accelerator to see if I can help you in any way, or you can reach me via email at alex@shiftstosuccess. com. Hopefully one day I will have the opportunity to support you on your entrepreneurial journey.

Thank you for taking the time to read *Police Officer to Entrepreneur*. If I have helped you make the smallest shift in your way of thinking, then I will have achieved my goal.

Review offer

If you feel as though this book would help other people, I would like to invite you to leave a review on Amazon, to help spread the word about *Police Officer to Entrepreneur*.

If you leave a review of the book on Amazon and send me a screenshot or link to your review, I will offer you a free 45-minute consultation, to help you go from 'police officer to entrepreneur', building or scaling your very own successful business.

Recommended Reading

All of these books are capable of creating mindset shifts.

Canfield, Jack, *The Success Principles*

Cardone, Grant, *Be Obsessed or Be Average*

Cardone, Grant, *The 10 x Rule*

Carnegie, Dale, *How to Win Friends and Influence People*

Collins, Jim, *Good to Great*

Covey, Stephen R., *The Seven Habits of Highly Effective People*

Coyle, Daniel, *The Talent Code*

Demarco, M.J., *The Millionaire Fastlane*

Demarco, M.J., *Unscripted*

Dweck, Caroline, *Mindset*

Gerber, Michael E., *The E Myth*

Grover, Tim S., *Relentless*

Hardy, Darren, *The Compound Effect*

Hardy, Darren, *The Entrepreneur Roller Coaster*

Harnish, Verne, *Scaling Up*

Hary Eker, T., *Secrets of the Millionaire Mind*

Hill, Napoleon, *The Law of Success*

Hill, Napoleon, *Success Through a Positive Mental Attitude*

Hill, Napoleon, *Think and Grow Rich*

Johnson, Kevin D., *The Entrepreneur Mind*

Keller, Peter, *The One Thing*

Kiyosaki, Robert, *Rich Dad, Poor Dad*

Kiyosaki Robert, *Rich Dad's Cash Flow Quadrant*

Knight, Phil, *Shoe Dog*

Maxwell, John C., *The 15 Invaluable Laws of Growth*

Maxwell, John C., *How Successful People Think*

Olsen, Jeff, *The Slight Edge*

Peters, Prof. Steve, *The Chimp Paradox*

Priestley, Daniel, *24 Assets*

Priestley, Daniel, *The Entrepreneur Revolution*

Priestley, Daniel, *Key Person of Influence*

Robbins, Mel, *The 5-Second Rule*

Schwartz, David J., *The Magic of Thinking Big*

Sunborn, *The Fred Factor*

Vaynerchuk, Gary, *Crush It*

Waite, Robin, *Take Your Shot*

Warrilow, John, *Built to Sell*

Acknowledgements

I'd like to thank:

PC Katie Saywell, PC Adam Doyle, PC Matthew Colburn, Carole Edwards and Robin Waite for all their valuable feedback as beta readers.

Sergeant David Egbokhan, Sergeant Lisa Murray, PC Francesca Coombes and Adam Wilkins for all their support while I was writing this book and their encouragement while I was developing Shifts to Success.

Rick Gannon, Dionne-Buckingham-Brown, Steven Thompson, Timothy Han, Josh Smith, Luke Vincent, Kul Mahay and PC Rob Webber for providing inspiring case studies.

My business mentors Simon Zutshi, Daniel Priestley, Andrew Priestley and James White for their outstanding guidance in bringing out my entrepreneurial spirit.

My accountability partner, Tara Halliday, for all her calls to ensure this book was being written.

My incredible publisher Rethink Press, especially Lucy McCarraher and Joe Gregory, for all their help and guidance in getting this book published.

My investors, joint venture partners and close friends Simon Platt, Sean Platt, John Viccars, and Natalie Viccars for all their support and encouragement.

Susan Haywood for her continued support and for treating me like a son.

My uncle, Mark Seery, a loving father figure, for helping me become the man I am today.

My best mate, Curtis Jackson, for all the laughs, adventures, and loyal support.

The Author

Alexander Seery is an author, speaker, successful entrepreneur, business coach and investor. With a deep passion for entrepreneurship and helping people realise their potential, Alex has studied entrepreneurs and businesses for the past six years.

At the age of twenty-four, he built his first company with zero start-up capital while working full-time in the police service. His business now generates a six-figure income and has accumulated over a million pounds' worth of assets. Alex has twice been featured in *YPN Magazine*, one of the UK's top business and investment publications.

Alex is the founder and CEO of Shifts to Success, a specialised business training company that exclusively supports ex- and serving police officers to build successful businesses with entrepreneurial ideas that are fun and respectable.

🌐 www.shiftstosuccess.com
f www.facebook.com/groups/ShiftstoSuccess
▶ Shifts to Success
📷 @alexanderseery
🐦 @shiftstosuccess